For Allan

Nothing is written.

Also by Steven Carter

Leopards in the Temple: Studies in American Popular Culture, Second Edition

TABLE OF CONTENTS

ACKNOWLEDGMENTS

Some of the essays in this book originally appeared in different form in the following periodicals and collections: "Foreword" under the title of "State of the Union: The Interrelations of Literature and Science" in the SPRING/SUMMER 1999 issue of *BRIDGES: An Interdisciplinary Journal of Theology, Philosophy, History, and Science* (ISSN 1042-2234; Monkton, Maryland); "Fields of Spacetime and the *I* in Charles Olson's *The Maximus Poems*"in the *Worcester Review* and in *American Literature and Science* ©1992 by Robert J. Scholnick, reprinted with permission of the University Press of Kentucky; "Mr. Duncan Meets Mr. Schrödinger" in *Studies in the Humanities*, reprinted in *The Poet's Voice/Second Series*; "Jack Spicer's Quantum Poetics" in *Literature and Science as Modes of Expression*, ed. Frederick Amrine (Boston: Kluwer Academic Publishers); "Reversible Syntax vs. Irreversible Time" in *Kwartalnik Neofilologiczny*, reprinted in *Language Quarterly*; "Ernest Hemingway and the Included Middle" in *CEA Critic*; "Hemingway's Canary for None: 'A Canary for One' " in *Prospero: Rivista di culture anglo-germanische*, reprinted in *Studia Anglia Posnaniensia: An International Review of English Studies*; "Krebs's Zero Summer: 'Soldier's Home' " in *Lubelski Materialy Neofilologiczne*; "Interrogating the Mirror: Double-crossings in 'The Killers' " in *Acta Neophilologica*, reprinted in *Language and Literature*; and "Rosencrantz and Guildenstern are Alive" in *The Hemingway Review*. Poems by Jack Spicer, ©1975 by the Estate of Jack Spicer, reprinted from *The Collected Books of Jack Spicer* with the permission of Black Sparrow Press.

⏮ ⏭

Much of Part I of *Bearing Across* originated as chapters of my Ph.D. dissertation at the University of Arizona. Especially helpful to me during my doctoral work in literature and science at Arizona were Patrick O'Donnell, my dissertation director, and Carl Tomizuka, my kind and patient mentor from the Department of Physics. In particular, I wish to honor the memory of the late Cecil Robinson, to whom I owe profound debts—both personal and professional—of friendship, advice, and encouragement.

In recent years, friends, colleagues, and support staff at Cal State Bakersfield have been no less helpful to me. Thanks to Professors Edwin J. Barton, Glenda A. Hudson, Michael Flachmann, and Lorna Clymer for conceptual and bibliographical suggestions regarding Part II of *Bearing Across*. Thanks also to Carolyn Alexander, Gloria Heaton, Sabine Westmoreland, and Alyssa Salkoff for their invaluable assistance.

Special thanks to Robert S. Frey, M.A., Editor/Publisher of *BRIDGES: An Interdisciplinary Journal of Theology, Philosophy, History, and Science*.

Foreword

In 1987, the Modern Language Association released a seminal volume of essays by various scholars entitled *Interrelations of Literature*. This intriguing baker's dozen of prolegomena included parallel discussions of literature and linguistics, literature and philosophy, literature and religion, literature and myth, literature and folklore, literature and sociology, literature and politics, literature and law, literature and psychology, literature and music, literature and the visual arts, literature and film, and literature and science. The essays collected in *Bearing Across* are concerned with the transdisciplinary poetics of the latter interrelation: the common epistemologies of literature and science.

The 1993 edition of the definitive *New Princeton Encyclopedia of Poetry and Poetics* devotes 11 double-columned pages to poetry and science alone. While the *Encyclopedia* mentions comparative critical studies that "consider the cognitive and social functions of the two fields,"[1] its discussions also focus on the historical competition between science and poetry as sovereign ways of knowing. This occasionally bitter rivalry, which traces its origin to Plato's supremely rational suspicion (in *The Republic*) of poetry's ability to convey truth, was updated in the 1950s in the form of a famous debate between C.P. Snow (for science) and F.R. Leavis (for literature). In a 1959 volume entitled *The Two Cultures and the Scientific Revolution*, Snow—every lit/sci scholar's *bête noire* —argued for science and the arts as inextricably separate entities. Contrawise, Leavis's "Richmond Lecture" of the same decade privileged literature as the *doyen* of modern intellectual life.

"Snow or Leavis?" Aldous Huxley asked ruefully—and rhetorically—in 1963: "The bland scientism of *The Two Cultures* or, violent and ill-mannered, the one-track, moralistic literalism of The Richmond Lecture?"[2] "If there were no other choice," Huxley continued,

> we should indeed be badly off. But happily there are middle roads, there is a more realistic approach to the subject [of literature and science] than was made by either of the two champions. And the two champions, let us remember, are not the only combatants in the field; they are merely, at this moment, the most notorious.[3]

One such level-headed combatant in or on the field of literature and science debates was the great critic I.A. Richards, who in 1935 anticipated both Snow and Leavis by asking,

> What is the truth in this matter? How is our estimate of poetry going to be affected by science? And how will poetry itself be influenced? The extreme importance which has in the past been assigned to poetry is a fact which must be accounted for whether we conclude that it was rightly assigned or not, and whether we consider that poetry will continue to be held in such esteem or not. It indicates that the case for poetry, whether right or wrong, is one which turns on momentous issues.[4]

Poets themselves have occasionally entered the fray. In an acerbic letter written in 1926, Hart Crane insisted that literature was literature and science was science, and never the twain *should* meet:

> When you ask for exact factual data (a graphic map of eternity?), ethical morality or moral classifications, etc., from poetry—you not only limit its goal, you ask its subordination to science, philosophy. Is it not equally logical to expect Stravinsky to bring his fiddles into dissent with the gravitation theories of Sir Isaac Newton?

Then Crane answers his own rhetorical question:

> They *are* in dissent with this scientist, as a matter of fact, and organically so; for the group mind that Stravinsky appeals to has already been freed from certain of the limitations of experience and consciousness that dominated both the time and the mind of Newton. Science (ergo all exact knowledge and its instruments of operation) is in perfect antithesis to poetry.[5]

Twenty years later, Crane's older contemporary William Carlos Williams took the opposite tack. In a talk given at the University of Washington, Williams became one of the first American poets not only to acknowledge but to *applaud* the possibility of meaningful correspondences between science (*e.g.*, physics) and poetry. In describing the unconventionality or rebelliousness of many contemporary poets as "similar to what must have been the early feelings of Einstein toward the laws of Isaac Newton in physics," Williams added:

> Thus [far] from being fixed, our prosodic values should be seen as only relatively true. Einstein had the speed of light as a constant—his only constant—what have we?[6]

Here, Williams neatly though unknowingly turned Hart Crane on his head, suggesting that poetry can and perhaps should look to science for epistemological models.[7]

The debate continues today.[8] In the October, 1997 issue of *Smithsonian*, John P. Wiley, Jr. indicates that the rift between intellectual disciplines is far from healed. In discussing John Brockman's book *The Third Culture*, one of many latter-day responses to the aging gauntlet thrown down by C.P. Snow, Wiley quotes the great quantum theorist Murray Gell-Mann: " '[T]here are people in the arts and humanities . . . who are proud of knowing very little about science and technology, or about mathematics.' " Wiley corroborates Gell-Mann's claim:

As a science editor, I run into that attitude all the time. People who have read a science story will say, with a proud smile: 'I didn't understand a word of it.' They say it in a tone of real satisfaction, as though happy they had not sullied themselves with the techno-geek side of life.[9]

It's not surprising, needless to say, that Wiley should come down hard on the side of science in this ongoing debate. He flatly concludes that "the most original, the most exciting work of the mind these days is being done by scientists . . . if anyone should be included in the ranks of the intellectuals, they should."[10]

Long before *The Two Cultures* appeared on the horizon, a goodly number of writers and thinkers had already begun to tease out discrete correspondences between science and the arts, including literature. *The New Princeton Encyclopedia* lists the following groundbreaking texts: A. N. Whitehead's *Science and the Modern World* (1925); L. Stevenson's *Darwin Among the Poets* (1932); I.A. Richards's *Science and Poetry* , 2nd ed. (1935), revised in 1970 as *Poetries and Sciences* ; A.O. Lovejoy's *The Great Chain of Being* (1936); D.G. James's *Scepticism and Poetry* (1937); A.M. Schmidt's *La Poesie scientifique en France au 16e siecle* (1938); A. Gode's *Natural Science in German Romanticism* (1941); M. S. Nicholson's *Newton Demands the Muse* (1946), *Science and Imagination* (1956), and *The Breaking of the Circle*, 2nd ed. (1962); F.W. Conner's *Cosmic Optimism: The Interpretation of Evolution by American Poets from Emerson to Robinson* (1949); D. Bush's *Science and English Poetry* (1950); H.H. Waggoner's *The Heel of Elohim: Science and Values in Modern American Poetry* (1950); Ifor Evans's *Literature and Science* (1954); J. Bronowski's *Science and Human Values* (1956); W.P. Jones's *The Rhetoric of Science: A Study of Scientific Ideas and Imagery in 18th-Century English Poetry* (1966); T.S. Kuhn's *The Structure of Scientific Revolutions*, 2nd ed. (1970) and *The Essential Tension* (1977); Hugh Kenner's *The Mechanic Muse* (1987); and W.D. Shaw's *The Lucid Veil* (1987).

The nineties has seen the publication of several collections of essays on literature, art, science, and technology, among them: *Literature and Technology*, edited by L. Schachterle and Mark L. Greenberg (1990); *American Literature and Science*, edited by Robert J. Scholnick (1992); *Literature and Science*, edited by Donald Bruce and Anthony Purdy (1994); and *Chaos and Order: Complex Dynamics in Literature and Science*, edited by N. Katherine Hayles (1994).

As interdisciplinary study has gained momentum over the decades, debates concerning the relationships between literature and science have become less territorial and/or value-judgmental and more sharply focused on the problem of method. "Method" can and does take many forms, of course, but let me suggest at the outset that, no matter what path they may choose to follow, interdisciplinary critics of literature who stray from the close readings of texts do so at their peril. In my view, to call *Gulliver's Travels* "a neurotic phantasy with coprophilia as its main content," with "other related neurotic characteristics accompanying the general picture of psychosexual infantilism,"[11] only serves to elucidate the prodigal in-house jargon brought *to* the text, not the text itself.

Scholars in the field of literature and science generally take one of two hermeneutical approaches. From one angle, the critic may explore ways in which certain writers *consciously* incorporate elements of key scientific discoveries into their fiction or poetry. From another angle, the critic attempts to describe certain epistemological models, or isomorphisms, shared by literature and science.

In American fiction, one of the best examples of a writer whose subject matter was profoundly influenced by science (or pseudo-science) was Frank Norris. In the 1890s, Norris attended the University of California at Berkeley for a brief time, where he took a course taught by Joseph LeConte, an (unfortunately) highly esteemed professor of natural history who once owned slaves and who believed in the genetic superiority of the white race. LeConte's eccentric readings of Darwin strongly influenced the impressionable Norris. Other influences on the young writer included the "criminal anthropologist" Cesare Lombroso and the French naturalist writer Emile Zola; both Lombroso and Zola helped to shape Norris's ideas concerning the role played by *instinct* in the evolution of individual human destinies (the title of one of Norris's minor works is *Vandover and the Brute*).

Note the recurrent beast imagery in the following scene from Norris's greatest novel, *McTeague:*

> The two men were grappling at each other wildly. The party could hear them panting and grunting as they labored and struggled. Their boots tore up great clods of turf. Suddenly they came to the ground with a tremendous shock. But even as they were in the act of falling, Marcus, like a very eel, writhed in the dentist's clasp and fell upon his side. McTeague crashed down upon him like the collapse of a felled ox.

And:

> Then followed a terrible scene. The brute that in McTeague lay so close to the surface leaped suddenly to life, monstrous, not to be resisted. He sprang to his feet with a shrill and meaningless clamor, totally unlike the ordinary bass of his speaking tones. It was the hideous yelling of a hurt beast, the squealing of a wounded elephant. . . . It was something no longer human; it was rather an echo from the jungle.[12]

What's significant here is not the intrinsic validity of a given scientific—or pseudo-scientific—theory, but the *influence* the theory has on the thinking of a writer like Frank Norris. Lombroso, like any number of scientists before and after him, has been thoroughly discredited in the decades following his death. Of more immediate interest, however, is the fact that the fictions of Frank Norris bear witness to the successful transubstantiation of bad science into good art—a subject that has received surprisingly little critical attention.

A world away from the human jungles of *McTeague* and *Vandover and the Brute*, the work of the great Irish poet William Butler Yeats also speaks to the direct influence of science on the thematics of literary productions. As Daniel Albright has shown,[13] Yeats had carefully studied Lyndon Bolton's *An Introduction to the Study of Relativity* "in order to see where modern physics fit into the historical gyres of *A Vision* ..." Concerning poems like "Sailing to Byzantium," Albright adds,

> [The] deconstructive tendencies [of quantum physics], its demotion of the universe into gaping unsolidities, seemed perfectly congruent with anarchy that attends the end of a millennium.[14]

In other words, Yeats's patented idea that *Things fall apart* was, for him, common to modern scientific and social revolutions alike.

While I believe that documenting one-to-one relationships between certain scientists and artists is an important critical endeavor, I also wish to draw attention to a second—and far more complex—transcultural phenomenon: the parallel presences of basic structures of human thought in the arts and sciences. It can be argued that such relationships actually tell us more about the complexities of cultural paradigms than do instances of direct influence. In parsing out the interrelationships between the texts of Max Planck and Franz Kafka, Valerie D. Greenberg observes,

> [T]he fact that Kafka and Planck are unlikely to have known of each other's existence *enhances* the notion of a distinctly textual dialogue between the scientific and the literary. (italics added)[15]

This dialogue comes in many forms and isn't restricted to the epistemes of science and literature. To take an important example from modern art, it's abundantly clear that Pablo Picasso and his circle of painters were intuitively aware of discoveries being made in the New Physics. Maurice Raynal remarked earlier in the century that

> one heard talk about the fourth dimension, non-Euclidean geometry, the theory of numbers and so forth, not that any of us knew much about mathematics . . . [T]hese conceptions seemed to sponsor ventures on the artists' part into strange lands beyond the frontier of conventional art . . .[16]

Carol C. Donley has pointed out that it was customary for modernist painters and poets to discuss their work in interdisciplinary terms—not in terms of specific influences but of a shared cultural vocabulary.[17] Thus Guillaume Apollinaire:

> Today, scientists no longer limit themselves to the three dimensions of Euclid. The painters have been led quite naturally, one might say by intuition, to preoccupy themselves with the new possibilities of spatial measurement which, in the language of the modern studios, are designated by the term, fourth dimension.[18]

As one of the premier spokesmen for the *Zeitgeist* that was Paris of the 'teens and twenties, Apollinaire firmly believed that correspondences such as these didn't necessarily originate in one discipline—in physics, in painting, or in literature—but that they *all* existed as part of a broad-based cultural paradigm, what Alfred North Whitehead called a climate of opinion.

Certain analogies between cultural phenomena are often suspect, and rightfully so, because in claiming too much they ultimately claim too little. John Adkins Richardson recalls Oswald Spengler's failed attempt to come up with a grand unified theory of history:

Spengler . . . maintained that, during the 17th century, analytic geometry, the music of the thorough-bass, and Baroque painting had all developed out of the 'same inspired ordering of an infinite world.' That may have been true, of course, but in Spengler it is all quite vaporous. . . . [Such] 'historicisms,' which assume for history an overall structure of movement of some kind, place hazards in the way of truth by insisting that each event be accommodated into the system at all costs.[19]

Richardson goes on to argue, however, that the search for meaningful parallels between disciplines can be a robust, viable enterprise:

We can speak safely of the unity of an age in terms of a consensus of ends, purposes, or ideals. And more often than not the coincidences of purpose that override, but do not abolish, distinctions among fields of interest tell us far more about the time than the disharmonies which produce conflict. Precisely such a coincidence of purpose is revealed in the parallels between nineteenth-century scientific views and attitudes common to Impressionist painters, literary Naturalists, and Positivists in philosophy.[20]

As long as we avoid the temptation to gloss over the very real differences and uniquenesses within the disciplines, finding affinities among them isn't an impossible—or even a chimerical—task. Indeed, it's an *obligatory* task, if we are to better understand basic structures of human thought, especially the ones that appear in different transdisciplinary contexts on a regular basis.

These basic structures take many different forms, or *isomorphisms*. While biologists use the term "isomorphism" to describe "a similarity in form, as in different kinds of organisms,"[21] interdisciplinary critics have appropriated it in their own attempts to pin down *specific patterns of recognition* shared by science, literature, and the arts.

Consider J. Bronowski's description of *the image* as a transdisciplinary isomorphism:

> You may have been told, you may still have the feeling, that $E=mc^2$ is not an imaginative statement. If so, you are mistaken. The symbols in that master-equation of the twentieth century—the E for energy, the m for mass, the c for the speed of light—are images for absent things or concepts, of exactly the same kind as the words 'tree' or 'love' in a poem. The poet John Keats was not writing anything which (for him at least) was not fundamentally different from an equation when he wrote,
>
> Beauty is truth, truth beauty,—that is all
> Ye know on earth, and all ye need to know.
>
> There is no difference in the use of such words as 'beauty' and 'truth' in the poem, and such symbols as 'energy' and 'mass' in the equation.[22]

Gillian Beer proposes this rich catena:

> Symmetry . . . simplicity, development, hierarchy, chance . . . [all] provide models, ideals and implied narratives in science as much as literature.[23]

Beer also sees in *relativism* an epistemological model for early twentieth-century literature and science:

> The relativizing of description is crucial both for advances in quantum mechanics and in modernism. Wave-particle duality and complementarity and [T.S. Eliot's] *The Waste Land* alike draw on this resource.[24]

Finally, Valerie D. Greenberg contributes *oscillation, recursion*, and *chiasmus* to the list of isomorphisms articulated across the disciplines of literature and science.[25]

In *Bearing Across*, I offer multiple perspectives on selected and specific interrelations of literature and science. Part I, entitled *Field, Quanta, Chaos*, is devoted to poetry; Part II, entitled *Complementarity*, to prose. Part I focuses on three different epistemes in the work of three different poets; Part II investigates the complexities of a single episteme in the work of one writer of fiction. Part I is largely—though not exclusively—concerned with the direct influences of scientific thought on individual writers and their work; Part II focuses on the role played by complementarity in the work of a writer—Ernest Hemingway—who, unlike Charles Olson, Robert Duncan, and Jack Spicer, evinces little, if any, direct knowledge of modern science.

I'll conclude by quoting a poet and two scientists on a subject of mutual concern: the limitations of language. All three are major players in *Bearing Across*, and all three share a common awareness of the inherent difficulties of describing "the real" in words.

Jack Spicer:

Words are what sticks to the real. We use them to push the real, to drag the real into the poem. They are what we hold on with, nothing else. They are as valuable in themselves as rope with nothing to be tied to.[26]

Werner Heisenberg:

All the words or concepts we use to describe ordinary physical objects, such as position, velocity, color, size, and so on, become indefinite and problematic if we try to use them on elementary particles.[27]

Niels Bohr:

When it comes to atoms, the language that must be used is the language of poetry.[28]

Swan Lake, Montana

NOTES

1. Alex Preminger and T.V.F. Brogan, eds., *The New Princeton Encyclopedia of Poetry and Poetics* (Princeton: Princeton University Press, 1993), p. 1121.

2. Aldous Huxley. *Literature and Science* (New Haven: Leet's Island Books, 1963), p.1.

3. *Ibid.*, p. 1.

4. I.A. Richards, *Poetries and Sciences* (New York: W.W. Norton, 1970), p. 21.

5. James Fenton, "Going Half the Way," *The New York Review of Books*, 23 October 1997, p. 33.

6. William Carlos Williams, *Selected Essays of William Carlos Williams* (New York: New Directions, 1954), p. 286.

7. As a poet who is acutely aware of the epistemological claims of science upon the modern imagination, William Carlos Williams has plenty of company. A survey of selected books of poetry written during the last 20 years alone includes these science-minded titles: *The New Physics; Red Shifts; Force Fields; Einstein's Brain; Parallax; New Science; Laughing at Gravity; Orrery; The Evolution of the Flightless Bird; Palladium; The Weight of Numbers; The Elements;* and *Darwin's Ark.*

8. The most thoroughgoing response to Snow in recent years is a collection of interdisciplinary essays defiantly titled, *One Culture: Essays in Science and Literature*, edited by George Levine (Madison: University of Wisconsin Press, 1987).

9. John P. Wiley, Jr., "Two Cultures—Never the Twain Shall Meet?," *Smithsonian*, October 1997, pp. 21-22.

10. *Ibid.*, p. 22.

    Wiley includes a Greek chorus of disgruntled scientists who speak out on the thorny issue of science versus the humanities:

    Paul Davies: Few intellectuals in Britain make any attempt to understand science, and clearly feel out of their depth with the issues being presented in recent books such as Stephen Hawking's *A Brief History of Time*. Some of the backlash seems to stem from a sense of helplessness in the face of this ignorance. 'I'm well educated,' they say, 'and I can't make sense of this. Therefore it must be bunk!'

    Richard Dawkins: I do feel somewhat paranoid about what I think of as a hijacking by literary people of the intellectual media.

    Nicholas Humphrey: There's terror among the British intelligentsia that culture has passed them by. They went to school, learned their classics, learned their English literature, thought of scientists as some kind of nerds. What went on in the chemistry or biology labs was beneath contempt for these intellectuals who were in touch with Plato and Aristotle and Julius Caesar. Such people, who are used to being dominant in our culture, are suddenly scared (22).

11.   These passages appeared in a 1942 issue of *The Psychoanalytic Review* and are quoted by Louis Landa in his essay, "Jonathan Swift," in Jonathan Swift, *Gulliver's Travels: An Annotated Text with Critical Essays*, ed. Robert A. Greenberg (New York: W.W. Norton, 1996), p. 275.

12.   Donald Pizer, ed., *McTeague: A Norton Critical Edition* (New York: W.W. Norton, 1977), pp. 132-33.

13.   Albright also points out that Thomas Hardy, "already over sixty years old,"

survived . . . to place Einstein as the terminus of a long series of shrinkers of mankind, including Copernicus and Darwin:

And now comes Einstein with a notion—
Not yet quite clear
To many here—
That there's no time, no space, no motion,
Nor rathe nor late,
Nor square nor straight,
But just a sort of bending-ocean. (13-14)

14.   Daniel Albright, *Quantum Poetics: Yeats, Pound, Eliot, and the Science of Modernism* (New York: Cambridge University Press, 1997), p. 13.

15.   Valerie D. Greenberg, *Transgressive Readings: The Texts of Franz Kafka and Max Planck* (Ann Arbor: University of Michigan Press, 1990), pp. 39-40.

16.   Maurice Raynal, *The Skira Modern Painting*, trans. Stuart Gilbert (Switzerland: World Publishing, 1960), p. 93.

17.   See Donley's pathbreaking Ph.D. dissertation, "Modern Literature and Physics: A Study of Interrelationships" (Kent State University, 1975), especially Chapters One and Two.

18.   Richard Ellmann and Charles Feidelson, eds., *The Modern Tradition* (New York: Oxford University Press, 1965), p. 116.

19.   John Adkins Richardson, *Modern Art and Scientific Thought* (Urbana: University of Illinois Press, 1971), p. xv.

20.   *Ibid.*, p. 3.

21.   This definition is taken from *The American Heritage Dictionary of the English Language.*

22.   J. Bronowski, *The Visionary Eye: Essays in the Arts, Literature, and Science* (Cambridge, Mass.: MIT Press, 1978), p. 21.

23.   Gillian Beer, "Problems of Description in the Language of Discovery," in *One Culture: Essays in Science and Literature*, ed. George Levine and Alan Rauch (Madison: University of Wisconsin Press, 1987), p. 46.

24.   Gillian Beer, "Wave Theory and the Rise of Literary Modernism," in *Realism and Representation: Essays on the Problem of Realism in Relation to Science, Literature, and Culture*, ed. George Levine (Madison: University of Wisconsin Press, 1993), p. 194.

25.   See Chapter One of *Transgressive Readings: the Texts of Franz Kafka and Max Planck.*

26.   Jack Spicer, *The Collected Books of Jack Spicer*, ed. Robin Blaser (Los Angeles: Black Sparrow Press, 1975), p. 25.

27.   Gary Zukav, *The Dancing Wu Li Masters: An Overview of the New Physics* (New York: Bantam Books, 1979), p. 21.

28.   Edward Harrison, *Masks of the Universe* (New York: Macmillan, 1985), p. 123.

Part I

Field, Quanta, Chaos

Fields of Spacetime and the *I* in
Charles Olson's *The Maximus Poems*

Or you can take an attitude, the creative vantage. . . . It involves a first act of physics. You can observe POTENTIAL and VELOCITY separately, have to, to measure THE THING. You get approximate results. They are usable enough if you include the Uncertainty Principle, Heisenberg's law that you learn the speed at the cost of exact knowledge of the energy and the energy at the loss of exact knowledge of the speed.

—Charles Olson, *Call Me Ishmael*

The notorious eclecticism of Charles Olson's[1] reading and scholarship owes a great deal to his interest in scientific texts. Unlike Robert Frost, who discovered after having written certain poems that he had intuitively embroidered into them concepts of quantum physics,[2] Olson was apparently directly influenced as a thinker and a poet by the work of a select group of scientists and mathematicians, including Bernard Riemann and Norbert Wiener. Thomas F. Merrill has pointed out that Olson relied heavily on Hermann Weyl's *The Philosophy of Mathematics and Natural Science* in his important 1957 essay, "Equal, That Is, to the Real Itself." It's Weyl's influence, Merrill suggests, that contributes to the scientific bias of Olson's argument, where "Olson spells out in remarkable detail, although in the confusing technical jargon of space-age physics, how he regards projective writing as an inevitable consequence of the same non-Euclidean 'redefinition of the Real' . . . that gave birth to relativity theory, quantum physics, and the whole conception of a continuous, as opposed to a classically discrete, universe." Merrill concludes his discussion of "Equal, That Is, to the Real Itself," with an interesting observation: "An apt metaphor for such a continuous reality is the electromagnetic field in which interrelated transformations of energy points take place. In such a field discrete

4

formulations, such as subject-object, cause-effect, and even mind-body, give way to the notion of flexible interplay between 'things among things.'"[3]

As we'll see, however, for the Charles Olson of *The Maximus Poems*, the quantum field heuristic represents less of a mere metaphor than it does a new poetics or rhetoric of verse. Kenith Levicoff Simmons has shown that, from the beginning of his career, Olson made it his business as a poet and a critic to parse out metonymic correspondences between modern science and literature—even the literature of the past:

> In poetry and poetics, we find the most penetrating understanding of the implications of quantum mechanics in the work of Charles Olson. Olson greeted Heisenberg's Uncertainty Principle without surprise and he immediately saw the relationship between Heisenberg's idea and nineteenth century literary ideas, specifically Keats's Negative Capability. Olson was delighted with Heisenberg's 'wonderful words to go with Keats's ambiguity. The Uncertainty Principle. Right out of the mouth of physics one can seize the condition Keats insisted a man must stay in the midst of.'[4]

At the conclusion of "Equal That Is, to the Real Itself," Olson celebrates the flexibility of another transdisciplinary episteme, the inertial field:

> Which it is [i.e., flexible], Einstein established, by the phenomena of gravitation, and the dependence of the field of inertia on matter. I take care to be inclusive, to enforce the point made at the start, that matter offers perils wider than man if he doesn't do what still today seems the hardest thing for him to do, outside of some art and science: to believe that things, and present ones, are the absolute conditions; but that they are so because the structures of the real are flexible, quanta do dissolve into vibrations, all does flow, and yet is there, to be made permanent, if the means are equal.[5]

For Olson, the structures of the real may carry over from the physical universe, the worlds of matter, to what in the title of another essay he calls the Human Universe, or the world(s) of consciousness. The two systems of matter and mind are intimately and inextricably bound up with each other. Olson's inspiration for such a holistic view of nature and man is Alfred North Whitehead, whose theory of "external objects" as physical qualities Olson applied to the mind itself:

> ... Whitehead's important corollary: that no event is not penetrated,
> in intersection or collision with, an eternal event. The poetics of such
> a situation are yet to be found out.[6]

Among other things, *The Maximus Poems* represents Olson's attempt to *find out* the poetics of a cross-pollination of scientific epistemologies with the language of verse.

Thomas F. Merrill isn't alone in borrowing from the language of quantum field theory to describe the esthetics of contemporary poets. A decade ago, Joseph N. Riddell provided a thumbnail sketch of one variety of postmodern poem. For him it is "a field located within known things, like the periodic table of elements, which compose a space housing an unknown disturbance, a dissonance, an undiscovered element that indicates the dynamics of the field."[7] It's highly likely that Riddell had in mind Charles Olson's earlier prolegomenon to the poetics of open form, the familiar "Projective Verse," in which Olson too defines poetry in terms of *"Composition by field*, as opposed to inherited line, stanza, over-all form, what is the 'old' base of the non-projective." What Riddell calls dynamics, Olson calls "the *kinetics* of the thing":

> A poem is energy transferred from where the poet got it (he will have
> several causations), by way of the poem itself to, all the way over to,
> the reader. . . . From the moment he ventures *into Field
> Composition*—puts himself in the open—he can go by no track other
> than the one the poem under hand declares, for itself.[8]

Olson's use of the word *kinetics* suggests that as early as 1950, when "Projective Verse" was written, he had a specific discipline in mind as a model for his theory of field, or open form. The discipline was, of course, physics, or, more accurately, post-Einsteinian physics. In a letter to his friend and publisher, Cid Corman, Olson insists that "the kinetics of contemporary physics [are] more healthful than"[9] the rigidities of either/or, man and world, psyche and cosmos, those separate categories inherited from the Greeks. The scientist Niels Bohr recalls the crucial distinction Olson is making when he suggests that for the contemporary quantum physicist as well, language markers inherited from the Greeks (cause and effect words like "because" and "therefore," for instance, which assume *a priori* a cause-and-effect cosmos) are inappropriate. For Bohr, "When it comes to atoms, the language that must be used is the language of poetry."[10] Both postmodern poetry and quantum physics, it would seem, have much to learn from each other.

Perhaps the most fertile epistemological common ground shared by the two disciplines is the field concept, which, according to the scientist Donna Haraway, "defined developments in dynamic instead of geographical terms. Every aspect of ontogeny had to be viewed in a double light, as the result of interactions between the material whole with its field properties on the one hand, and the material parts on the other."[11] The essence of Haraway's definition is to be found in the phrase, "a double light." It's the *doubleness* of field that creates difficulty in understanding its ambiguities. As the physicist B.K. Ridley has observed, "The total energy of a moving particle, rest-mass plus kinetic, is . . . nothing but the total energy of its own electromagnetic field.[12] To say that a particle is both a particle *and* the field that it inhabits makes no sense in classical physics, which, as Charles Olson suggests, is epistemologically far less relevant to the postmodern poet than is quantum physics.

Projectivist verse is a poetry of relationships. As Karl Malkoff has written, "The domain of the Projectivist poem is the point of intersection between inner and outer realities."[13] *The Maximus Poems* shouldn't be read merely as a series of discrete, watertight expressions of Charles Olson's visions of Gloucester, Massachusetts, past and present; rather, *Maximus* expresses meanings only as a matrix of relationships among the poems. These matrices, or interactions, include the voice(s) of Maximus, who moves freely in space and time throughout the sequences of poems; the town and people of Gloucester, Massachusetts; and the historical personages who appear and disappear in the shimmering spacetime field of *The Maximus Poems*.

The epistemology which Malkoff uses to describe Projectivist verse is also used by physicists to define field.[14] A subatomic particle is nothing but a focus of relationships between fields. As far as *Maximus* is concerned, the key feature of field poetics is the classical quantum paradox, or the non-Aristotelian habit of mind that suggests that reality can be two or more different things at the same time. The physicist Gary Zukav points out that "Quantum field theory is, of course, an outrageous contradiction in terms. A quantum is an indivisible whole. It is a small piece of something, while a field is a whole area of something. A 'quantum field' is the juxtaposition of two irreconcilable concepts. In other words, it is a paradox. It defies our categorical imperative that something be either *this* or *that*."[15]

Three fields of action in *Maximus* create this paradox, defying Aristotelian logic and linearity by interacting with each other "*instantaneously* and at one single point in space instantaneously and locally."[16] The fields of *Maximus* may be defined as time, space, and the *I* of the sequence; *The Maximus Poems* represents the interactions of these three fields. Each of the three poems I'll discuss exhibits all three fields of action; "Letter 15," however, emphasizes the field of time, whereas "On First Looking out through Juan de la Cosa's Eyes" emphasizes the field of space.

8

In "The Twist," fields of spacetime coalesce around the *I*, or the speaker (Maximus), who emerges as a fully articulated consciousness. Although three poems represent a necessarily small sampling of the considerable riches of *Maximus*, each poem included here fully expresses at least one of the three central themes of the work: the rapaciousness and waste that Olson associates with twentieth-century American capitalism; the close personal and mythical identification of the speaker with the fishing town of Gloucester; and Maximus's wider identification with the past, wherein Gloucester becomes not simply a city, or *polis*, to be discovered, but a means of discovery of what it means to be Maximus, or man.

"Letter 15" from Maximus begins with a remembrance of things past, as the speaker corrects the historical record concerning the fate of a ship called the *Putnam*. The narrative dramatizes the difficulty of keeping the truth alive through time: "The whole tale, as we have had it, from his son, goes by the board. The son seems to have got it thirty-five years after the event from a sailor who was with the father on that voyage (to Sumatra, and Ile de France, cargo: shoes). This sailor apparently (he was twenty years older than the captain) was the one who said, that night they did get in, 'Our old man goes ahead as if it was noonday.' He must have been 85 when he added the rest of the tale."[17] The theme of the mutability of memory—and therefore of history—is reinforced elsewhere in *Maximus* when the speaker declares, "History is the memory of time" (*Maximus*, 116). This theme in the opening section of "Letter 15" also prefigures the technique of many of the poems to come. Even as memory is slippery—an old man's reminiscences of a ship in Gloucester—so is time itself slippery. As Sherman Paul has written,

> Maximus tells us that his poem will not make us comfortable because it does not follow a linear track to a foreseen destination. In addressing his method, he reminds us of his weaving and of the indivisibility of his concerns—and of his materials, since everything, as with the bird, everything (immediate observation, document, recollection, dream, myth) is the common real material of his poem.

In the field there are no boundaries . . . the field he enters is not a
subject but the reality he fronts, the place of his attentions. . . . His
subject, if he may be said to have one, is man-within-the-field.[18]

In "Letter 15," the indivisibility of Maximus's concerns is dramatized, not *in*, but *as*, a field of time. The adventure of the *Putnam* cannot be reduced to a single event that happened in space or time. Instead, Olson distributes authority for the truth of the ship's fate among several narrators and audiences—Maximus himself, the *we* of the passage, the son, the sailor, and the distant father. It's a technique that recalls the radical narrative strategies of Joseph Conrad in *Heart of Darkness* and William Faulkner in *The Sound and the Fury*, among others.

Significantly, Olson's technique in "Letter 15" also recalls Einstein's definition of fields of energy: "Matter which we perceive is merely nothing but a great concentration of energy in very small regions. We may therefore regard matter as being constituted by the regions of space in which the field is extremely intense . . . . There is no place in this new kind of physics both for the field and matter for the field is the only reality."[19] For Olson the rhetorician of verse, Einstein's physical field represents more than a phenomenon that is restricted to the physical cosmos. Nor is field for Olson just a metaphor for postmodern poetics. Rather, in Olson's view, human consciousness *itself* is a field, whether it's expressed in a scientific or in a poetical view of things: "At root (or stump) of what is, is no longer THINGS but what happens BETWEEN things, these are the terms of the reality contemporary to us—and the terms of what we are."[20]

But if field as Einstein defines it denotes a unity in space, for Olson in "Letter 15" it also denotes a unity in time. Olson's attempt to orchestrate a unity between time present and time past in the human cosmos of Gloucester becomes clearer if we examine a quantum model that theoretical physicist David Bohm uses to describe the implicate order of the physical cosmos:

> [E]ach local clock of a given level exists in a certain region of space and time [i.e., the field] which is made up of still smaller regions, and so on without limit. We shall see that the universality of the quantum of action, h, may be obtained at all levels, if we assume that each of the above *sub-regions* contains an effective clock of a similar kind, related to the other effective clocks of its level in a similar way, and that this effective clock structure continues indefinitely with the analysis of space and time into sub-regions.[21]

Bohm's thought-experiment with ideal clocks is meant to suggest the universality of the quantum of action: that is, a truth about space and time that exists in both micro- and macroscopic physical reality.

In like manner, Charles Olson's use of time in "Letter 15" and elsewhere in *The Maximus Poems* represents *an attempt to devise a quantum of action in language*. Olson achieves his quantum of action (h in the physical cosmos) by searching out in *Maximus*—in the ordinary lives of men and women who populate the poems—what is common to all times and places, dividing time as he does so into conventional sub-regions (the seventeenth and twentieth centuries, say), and then using these universal human constants (h might as well stand for human) to erase the boundaries of the sub-regions, of time altogether, creating a sense of what in the physical cosmos Bohm simply calls wholeness.

In Part II of "Letter 15," for example, Maximus leaps from the historical account of the *Putnam* to a conversation in the present with poet Paul Blackburn, who has accused Maximus/Olson of twisting the poem, i.e., beating around the bush, leaving the subject for bizarre tangents. Olson/Maximus agrees with Blackburn, and then replies cryptically, "I sd., Rhapsodia . . ." (*Maximus*, 72). Olson knew that the word rhapsodist comes from *rhaptein*, which, as Don Byrd points out, means "to sew, to stitch together, and *aidein*, to sing. The poet is a stitcher of songs."[22] The songs of Maximus in part comprise the tangents of the poem that Blackburn objects to; and yet the tangents are also the poems. It is Maximus who sings them, even if they are written by someone else—John Smith, for example. Smith, as a historical personage, is part of the field of *The Maximus Poems*. Maximus, the *I* of the poem where intersecting fields of time and space meet, *is also the field*. That is to say, Maximus subsumes John Smith:

> The winters cold, the Summers heat
>   alternatively beat
> Upon my bruised sides, that rue
>   because too true
> That no releefe can ever come
>   But why should I despaire
>   being promised so faire
> That there shall be a day of Dome [*Maximus*, 74]

Smith's poem is a testament of self, but it's also another voice in the Greek chorus that constitutes the testament of Maximus. Thus, historical time for Olson is an illusion; "Letter 15" ends in a sudden, bitter shift to the present age, a wrinkle in the intersecting fields of the poem, thanks to one word. "ADVERTISEMENTS" forms part of the title of a book by John Smith. In present-day American culture, ADVERTISEMENTS leads to this:

> o Republic, o
> Tell-A-Vision, the best
> is soap. The true troubadours
> are CBS. Melopoeia
>   is for Cokes by Cokes out of
>   Pause
>
> IV
> (o Po-ets, you
> should getta
> job [*Maximus*, 75]

In "Letter 15," linear time is subsumed by the universality of the temporal quantum of action: in this case, greed. In Section II of the poem, Maximus points out that John Smith was rejected for the job of navigator by the pilgrims in favor of Captain Myles Standish. For Maximus, Smith is a man of integrity, and yet, even in his time, the seeds of American corporate venality can be detected; the decision to appoint Standish as navigator was made "to save charges," as Smith himself wrote bitterly.[23]

In the above references to both contemporary advertising and pragmatic American attitudes toward good-for-nothing poets, Maximus is quick to dramatize equivalent examples of self-interest and shortsightedness. From the point of view of a crassly materialistic capitalist society, linear time, therefore, has made little difference between Smith's day and our own. In other words—to borrow Einstein's terminology above—greed appears in "Letter 15" as a region of Maximus's consciousness where the field of time becomes extremely intense; more than three centuries of chronological time melt away in favor of a concentration, not of physical, but of human psychic energy, whose localized manifestations in the seventeenth and twentieth centuries appear with an American twist, and are similarly perverse. Thus a precise correspondence exists between the manner in which physicists (Einstein and Bohm) perceive the implicate orders of energy fields, and the manner in which a poet (Olson) perceives the intricate orders of the human psyche, whose representations in *The Maximus Poems* are interwoven with the tissues and textures of post-Einsteinian spacetime.

In the poem, "On First Looking out through Juan de la Cosa's Eyes," the explorer la Cosa emerges as a hero of *The Maximus Poems* because, like Maximus himself, he presents for the reader a mythological present. But the true value of la Cosa's voyages in *Maximus* is spatial: his centrality as a human being is expressed by the poet in terms of literal fields of space. Literal, because it is Juan de la Cosa's map of the world which makes of the world a whole for the first time in history. La

Cosa captained the *Niña* in 1492, but is better known as chief chart maker for Christopher Columbus. Eight years after the voyage to the New World, la Cosa produced his mappenmunde of the Old and New Worlds, inscribed "Juan de la Cosa la fizo en el puerto de s:mjª en ano de 1500."[24] For Charles Olson, la Cosa's map is a mythological model for wholeness as well, for in it all men share the same space; in the poem the map becomes a spatial metaphor for human brotherhood. It also serves as a model for Maximus, the *I* who transcends space in "la Cosa's Eyes" in the same fashion as the *I* of "Letter 15" who transcends time. Maximus says ecstatically,

> . . . before la Cosa, nobody
> could have
> a mappenmunde [*Maximus*, 81]

Later in *The Maximus Poems*, the *I* takes his place as a settler in la Cosa's mappenmunde, when he declares, "I am making a mappenmunde. It is to include my being" (*Maximus*, 201). The physical space of la Cosa's world thus dovetails with the spirituality of Maximus's being; in space now, as he does in time in "Letter 15," Maximus becomes the field *and* the man within the field. As Olson says elsewhere, "The littlest [man within the field of history] is the same as the very big [the field of history], if you look at it."[25] The lineaments of physical space dwell within the psyche of each man who is contained by space, because physical space is also contained (i.e., perceived by) each man. La Cosa's mappenmunde is thus psychic *and* physical, a sort of Mercator's projection of inner and outer spaces that coexist as a simultaneous field.

As always in *The Maximus Poems*, in "la Cosa's Eyes" the fields of space, time, and the speaker's *I* overlap; as Don Byrd correctly observes, "Space and history [in] the post-Einsteinian cosmos of [Maximus] are only different manifestations of the same order."[26] For Einstein, of course, space and time aren't separate quantities; they both constitute linked phenomena in a universal continuum called spacetime.

For Maximus/la Cosa, the world is no longer flat, for the mappenmunde remakes the frightening world out there, a world of "mermaids and monsters" (*Maximus*, 82), into curved space, a terrestrial precursor of universal curved space:

> Respecting the earth, he said,
> it is a pear, or,
> like a round ball upon a part of which there is a prominence
> like a woman's nipple, this protrusion
> is the highest & nearest to
> the sky [*Maximus*, 83]

In "On First Looking out through Juan de la Cosa's Eyes," a reader may understand, perhaps for the first time in *The Maximus Poems*, the literal uses of space on the page. Entire pages of *The Maximus Poems* are left purposefully blank. It's as if pure spacetime, pure becoming, takes over where words suddenly fail Maximus. And yet the spaces between words create as much meaning as the words themselves. Even as the holes in Henry Moore's sculptures are meant by the artist to be seen, or as the silences in John Cage's musical compositions are meant by the composer to be heard, so the white spaces on the pages of *The Maximus Poems* are meant by the poet to be read. Olson's white spaces represent future time which, like the past, is encysted by the Bergsonian perpetual *now* of the poems.

Olson's syntax also depends for its meaning upon the open spaces in *The Maximus Poems*. It's a fractured syntax, a fractured typography, floating like jetsam in the sea off Gloucester, the sea of spacetime that Olson observes through Maximus's colossal memory, which he defines as the history of time:

> No worms. Storms,
> Ladies &
> to the bottom of the,
> husbands, & wives,
> little children lost their [*Maximus*, 84]

Here, Maximus's syntax is in the perpetual process of becoming a sentence, i.e., a complete thought. Similarly, Olson's characterization of Maximus himself represents a process of becoming a sentient whole. Of course, this process of becoming, of succeeding generations lost and found offshore in the Atlantic ocean, is also the subject of the passage.

The theme of "On First Looking out through Juan de la Cosa's Eyes," therefore, is continuity: the continuity of the curved space of la Cosa's mappenmunde which, in Gloucester's flower ceremony in August, translates into a magnetic chain of memory that links the living with the dead:

> . . . each summer, at the August full,
> they throw flowers, which, from the current there, at the Cut,
> reach the harbor channel, and go
> these bouquets (there are few, Gloucester, who can afford florists' prices)
> float out
>   you can watch them go out into,
> the Atlantic [*Maximus*, 84]

The field of the dead and the living in *The Maximus Poems* is meshed by the flower ceremony, which, in "Letter 36" as well, exists to create continuity:

> the flowers
> turn
> the character of the sea. The sea jumps
> the fate of the flower. The drowned men are undrowned
> in the eddies
>   of the eyes
>   of the flowers
>   opening
>   the sea's eyes [*Maximus*, 157]

The syntactical mixing of flowers, eyes of the people, and the drowned men of Gloucester represents a direct attack in language on the illusion of spatial and temporal separateness in the world. Indeed, the very concept of field denies a reality of bits and pieces altogether. By embracing Gloucester, the Cut, Dogtown, the sea, the drowned men, and flowers tossed into the waves by huddled women and children stitching the field of spacetime together with remembrance, la Cosa's mappenmunde ultimately meshes the temporal field of "Letter 15" with the spatial field of "On First Looking out through Juan de la Cosa's Eyes."

"The Twist," the third major poem in the fields of *The Maximus Poems*, is also one of the most personal poems. In it the *I* of Maximus, the being in la Cosa's mappenmunde, takes his place in the spacetime field of "Letter 15" and "On First Looking out through Juan de la Cosa's Eyes." "The Twist" bears a striking contrast to "la Cosa's Eyes," however, because it represents la Cosa's mappenmunde turned inside out: now we have Maximus's naked being, the personal Maximus, the man in the field. In fact, as Don Byrd has pointed out, Olson's flipover of world to man in the world makes "The Twist" resemble a kind of moebius strip of words,[27] and reminds us again that the Einsteinian space of *The Maximus Poems* isn't linear but curves back on itself. Thus, la Cosa's stormy coast becomes, in "The Twist,"

> . . . my inland waters
> (Tatnuck Sq. and the walk
> from the end of the line
> to Paxton, for May-flowers
> or by the old road to Holden
> after English walnuts [*Maximus*, 86]

Following la Cosa's map, a man who departs from Gloucester will eventually curve his way backward to the inland waters where he began. The discovery of a new world, therefore, becomes a simultaneous discovery of self, of Maximus's being suddenly incarnated among the May-flowers and ancient walnut trees of Gloucester.

As we saw in the poem dedicated to him, the fact that la Cosa (who smelled these same May-flowers centuries ago) is dead, is immaterial. For both time and space are dissolved in "The Twist," and Maximus—who's an echo of la Cosa himself—is the locus of the two, the intersection of the fields. "The Twist" is purely subjective: the *I* is fluid everywhere in the poem, not as one identity separate from the field of objects, memories, and reflections, but as a chorus:

> I went home
> as fast as I could,
>
> the whole Cut
> was a paper village my Aunt Vandla
> had given me, who gave me,
> each Christmas,
> such toys
>
> As dreams are, when the day
> encompasses. They tear down
> the Third Ave. El. Mine stays,
> as Boston does, inches up.
> I run my trains
> on a monorail, I am seized
> —not so many nights ago—
> by the site of the river
> exactly there at the Bridge
>
> where it goes out & in
>
> I recognize
> the country ... [*Maximus*, 89]

As the physiognomy of the moebius strip, and as a metaphor for Einsteinian curved space, the concept of *in* and *out* in "The Twist" is fundamentally important for an understanding of *The Maximus Poems* as a whole. The meandering of the river exists in time as well as space: "—not so many nights ago—" unites the boy Maximus and the man Maximus remembering, and suddenly spills into the spatial "out & in" of the river. In Einsteinian space, the concept of *inness*, as opposed to the concept of *outness*, makes no sense at all; like the surfaces of the moebius strip, both *in* and *out* are made of what the particle physicist Fritjof Capra calls inseparable energy patterns.[28] For Olson, as for the contemporary physicist, there can be no isolation of events in the universe of space and time. Olson demonstrates this Einstein-inspired truism in both "la Cosa's Eyes" and "The Twist." La Cosa's mappenmunde is the *out* of "The Twist," whose *in* is the map of Gloucester retraced in the personal memory of Maximus. "La Cosa's Eyes" ends with the lines,

> On ne doit aux morts nothing
> else than
> la verité [*Maximus*, 85]

which translate, *We owe the dead nothing else than the truth.*

> "The Twist" ends with the lines,

> the whole of it
> coming,
> to this pin-point
> to turn
> in this day's sun,
> in this veracity
> there, the waters of several of them the roads
> here, a blackberry blossom [*Maximus*, 90]

The historical veracity we owe to the memory of the dead, to la Cosa himself, twists structurally on the moebius strip of "The Twist" to become the veracity of personal observation and discovery, exemplified by the poignant care with which the poem names Maximus's photographic memories of flowers.

It's chimerical to ask of any epic narrative that it attain perfect unity; indeed, the concept of unity itself is anathema to postmodern poetics. As many critics have noticed, there are real differences between *The Maximus Poems* of 1960 and *Maximus IV, V, VI*, published in 1968.[29] Nonetheless, if seeing *The Maximus Poems I-VI* as all of a piece is a matter of infinite hope, unity may be perceived in certain elegant clusters of poems within the larger work. The poetics of field offer a skeleton key to the interrelationships among the lyrics of at least one such cluster in *The Maximus Poems*. For in "The Twist," that little masterpiece of open form, the field of space, time, and the *I* of Maximus is complete; the passion of historical memory in "Letter 15" embraces the floating flowers of grieving women in "la Cosa's Eyes" and harmonizes in the moebius strip of "The Twist" with Maximus's sympathies for la Cosa, for Gloucester's own sailors, and for the waters of his own past in a village by the sea.

NOTES

1. Charles Olson *(1910-1970)* was the leading proponent of post-Poundian open form poetics that emerged on the American cultural scene after World War II. In the late forties and fifties, Olson taught and served as rector at Black Mountain College, an experimental school in North Carolina whose occasional faculty included Eric Bentley, Alfred Kazin, Robert Creeley, Robert Duncan, Ben Shahn, Josef Albers, and Robert Motherwell. Olson was the author of many volumes of prose and poetry, including *Call Me Ishmael, Mayan Letters, Human Universe and Other Essays, The Distances, O'Ryan, In Cold Hell, In Thicket, X & Y*, and, of course, *The Maximus Poems.*

    —from "Projective Verse":

    ONE PERCEPTION MUST IMMEDIATELY AND DIRECTLY LEAD TO ANOTHER PERCEPTION. It means exactly what it says, is a matter of, at all points (even, I should say, of our management of daily reality as of the daily work) get on with it, keep moving, keep in, speed, the nerves, their speed, the perception, theirs, the acts, the split second acts, the whole business, keep it moving as fast as you can, citizen. And if you also set up as a poet, USE USE USE the process at all points, in any given poem always, always one perception must must must MOVE, INSTANTER, ON ANOTHER!

2. See Guy Rotella, "Comparing Conceptions: Frost and Eddington, Heisenberg, and Bohr," *American Literature* 59 (1987): 168-89.

3. Thomas F. Merrill, *The Poetry of Charles Olson: a Primer* (Newark, Del.: University of Delaware Press, 1982), pp. 57-58.

4. Kenith Levicoff Simmons, "Old Maids and the Domination of the Sea: Robert Duncan, Stan Brakhage, and Robert Kelly on the Self in Context" (Ph.D. diss., University of Wisconsin, Madison, 1978), p. 11. The quotation from Olson may be found in Ann Charters, ed., *The Special View of History* (Berkeley: Oyez Press, 1970), p. 39.

5. Charles Olson, *Selected Writings*, ed. Robert Creeley (New York: New Directions, 1966), p. 52.

6. Charles Olson, *The Maximus Poems IV, V, VI* (London: Cape Goliard/Grossman, 1968), 79. Qtd. in Paul Christensen, *Charles Olson: Call Him Ishmael* (Austin: University of Texas Press, 1979), p. 138.

7. Joseph N. Riddell, *The Inverted Bell* (Baton Rouge: Louisiana State University Press, 1974), p. 14.

8. Olson, *Selected Writings*, p. 16.

9. Charles Olson, *Letters for Origin*, ed. Albert Glover (New York: Cape Goliard, 1970), p. 51.

10. Edward Harrison, *Masks of the Universe* (New York: Macmillan, 1985), p. 123.

11.   Donna Jean Haraway, *Crystals, Fabrics, and Fields* (New Haven: Yale University Press, 1976), p. 178.

12.   B.K. Ridley, *Time, Space, and Things* (New York: Penguin, 1976), p. 120.

Such radical interpretations of the physical world aren't limited to scientists (or poets). In a chapter devoted to Claude Monet in his book *The Innocent Eye*, Roger Shattuck suggests that visions of the artist and the scientist may correspond at the most fundamental levels of existence:

> Monet approached the painting of *matter itself*, matter so thoroughly penetrated by his eye as to appear as fields, as lines of force, dissolved into energy in a way comparable to Einstein's scientific insight that matter is convertible into energy.

Shattuck adds that Monet's vision of the heart of things, while dazzlingly beautiful, is also terrifying:

> The security of appearance screens us from the fluctuating field [James Clerk] Maxwell tried to diagram, from the elementary particles that will not hold still, and from the dizzying dance of it all on our own retinas. The world is in constant flux, yes, not on its surface but behind, in its depths. Here is the abyss. Monet attested to its power over him by the galvanic strength with which he clung to 'what he saw,' to nature. (New York: Farrar, Straus & Giroux, 1984, pp. 232, 239.)

13.   Karl Malkoff, *Escape from the Self* (New York: Columbia University Press, 1977), p. 66.

14.   In *Quantum Mechanics and Experience*, David Z. Albert offers the following extended definition of a quantum field:

What goes on in relativistic quantum theories is that one imagines that there is an infinitely tiny physical system permanently located at every single mathematical point in the entirety of space; one imagines (that is) that there is literally an infinite array of such systems, one for each point. And each one of those infinitely tiny systems is stipulated to be a quantum-mechanical system. And each one of them is stipulated to interact in a particular way with each of its neighbors. And the complete array of them is called the field. (Cambridge, Mass.: Harvard University Press, 1992, pp. 59-60).

N. Katherine Hayles sees the field model, as I do, as an interdisciplinary paradigm. In her excellent study, *The Cosmic Web: Scientific Field Models and Literary Strategies in the Twentieth Century*, Hayles applies field dynamics to modern fictional texts:

> Since any statement in a field model can be made to refer to itself if the statement is part of the field that the model posits, statements have the potential to become self-referential, a realization as central to Godel's theorem [in mathematics] as it is to [Jorge Luis] Borges's fictions. The supposition that there

> is a speaking subject separate from the object that is being spoken about also becomes problematic, and generates an uneasiness that is as apparent in most modern interpretations of the [Heisenberg] Uncertainty Relation as in [Thomas] Pynchon's *Gravity's Rainbow.*

Hayles adds Einsteinian cosmology to the mix:

> Another assumption that becomes paradoxical in a field model is the premise that it is possible to establish an unambiguous time-line for spatially separated events, a conception whose unraveling is as important to relativity theory as it is to [Vladimir] Nabokov's *Ada.* (Ithaca: Cornell University Press, 1984, pp. 21-22.)

What Hayles calls the "unraveling" of linear time as a classical measurement for "spatially separated events" is part and parcel of the structural dynamics—i.e., the field—of Olson's *The Maximus Poems.*

15.   Gary Zukav, *The Dancing Wu Li Masters: An Overview of the New Physics* (New York: Bantam, 1979), p. 200.

16.   *Ibid.,* p. 199.

17.   Charles Olson, *The Maximus Poems,* ed. George F. Butterick (Berkeley: University of California Press, 1983), p. 71. All subsequent references to this edition as *Maximus* in text.

18.   Sherman Paul, *Olson's Push* (Baton Rouge: Louisiana State University Press, 1978), p. 142.

19.   Qtd. in Milic Capek, *The Philosophical Impact of Contemporary Physics* (New York: Van Reinhold Nostrand Company, 1961), p. 319.

20.   Charles Olson, *Human Universe and Other Essays,* ed. Donald Allen (New York: Grove Press, 1967), p. 123. Qtd. in Robert von Hallberg, *Charles Olson: the Scholar's Art* (Cambridge, Mass.: Harvard University Press, 1978), p. 97.

21.   David Bohm, *Wholeness and the Implicate Order* (London: Routledge and Kegan Paul, 1980), p. 98.

22.   Don Byrd, *Charles Olson's Maximus* (Urbana: University of Illinois Press, 1980), p. 91.

23.   See George F. Butterick, *A Guide to* The Maximus Poems *of Charles Olson* (Berkeley: University of California Press, 1978), p. 103.

24.   See *Ibid.,* pp. 115-16.

25.   Qtd. in Paul, *Olson's Push,* p. 163.

26.   Byrd, *Charles Olson's Maximus,* p. 89.

27.   *Ibid.*, p. 90.

28.   Fritjof Capra, *The Tao of Physics* (New York: Bantam, 1977), p. 69, qtd. in N. Katherine Hayles, *The Cosmic Web*, p. 19.

29.   See Merrill, *The Poetry of Charles Olson*, pp. 193-94.

Mr. Duncan Meets Mr. Schrödinger

This music of men's speech that has its verity in the music of the inner structure of nature is clearly related to that beauty of mathematics that Schrödinger and Dirac feel relates to the beauty of the inner structure of the physical universe.
—Robert Duncan, "Towards an Open Universe"

[T]he isolated knowledge obtained by a group of specialists in a narrow field has in itself no value whatsoever, but only in its synthesis with all the rest of knowledge and only inasmuch as it really contributes in this synthesis something toward answering the demand, . . . 'Who are we?'
—Erwin Schrödinger, *Science and Humanism*

In his seminal essay, "Towards an Open Universe," Robert Duncan[1] observes that "[a]tomic physics has brought us to the threshold"[2] of a new epistemology. From the very beginning of his career as a poet, Duncan made it abundantly clear that physics and the other sciences are intimately connected with his poetry. Duncan sets out to explain this connection in "Towards an Open Universe": "Our consciousness, and the poem as a supreme effort of consciousness, comes in a dancing organization between personal and cosmic identity."[3] Among the great quantum physicists of this century, Duncan turns most often to Erwin Schrödinger for interdisciplinary corroboration of his poetics:

What gnosis of the ancients transcends in mystery the notion Schrödinger brings us of an aperiodic structure in *What is Life?*: '. . . the more and more complicated organic molecule in which every atom, every group of atoms, plays an individual role, not entirely equivalent to that of others.' *Living matter evades the decay to equilibrium,* Schrödinger titles a section of his essay in 1944. 'When is a piece of matter said to be alive?' he asks, and answers, 'When it goes on "doing something," moving, exchanging material with its environment.'

Duncan then switches the discussion back to poetics and poetry: "What interests me here is that this picture of an intricately articulated structure, a form that maintains a disequilibrium or lifetime—whatever it means to the biophysicist—to the poet means that life is by its nature orderly and that the poem might follow the primary processes of thought and feeling, the immediate impulse of psychic life."[4] Duncan's and Schrödinger's interest in aperiodic structures which evade "the decay to equilibrium" is shared by another quantum physicist, David Bohm, who also asks, "At which point can we say that there is a sharp distinction between what is alive and what is not? Clearly, a molecule of carbon dioxide that crosses a cell boundary into a leaf does not suddenly 'come alive' nor does a molecule of oxygen suddenly 'die' when it is released in the atmosphere." Bohm concludes that life has to be interpreted "in some sense" as a "totality, including plant and environment."[5]

When Duncan refers to Schrödinger's biophysics as aperiodic, he is thinking simultaneously of poetic form. Sherman Paul defines the essential *esthetic* distinctions between aperiodicity and

> periodic structure, which originates in the balanced rhythms of day and night, the tides, the pulse beat; which has formal correlatives in 'rhyming lines and repeated meter'; which Duncan says . . . expresses our desire to return to 'the inertia of uncomplicated matter.' Periodic forms are entropic, are associated with 'the chemistry of death.'
> . . . Like a tree, like an aperiodic poem; both are complicated forms in which the elements, like atoms, play 'individual role[s].' Aperiodic forms, then, are tropic; they resist entropy with ergs, with desire.[6]

Robert Duncan's interest in the interrelationships between aperiodic structures in poetry and in science extends beyond biophysics to include quantum mechanics. When in a 1977 interview he tells George Bowering and Robert Hogg that "you have to go back and back and back and refresh your mind with the resources of science," he's thinking in particular of the ways in which quantum physics can offer epistemological alternatives to the inertia of periodic or entropic systems of language. Duncan adds, "I've been on that one way [i.e., eschewing the model of syllable as subatomic particle], and it [Duncan's poetics *circa* 1977] may only come from the potency that's in the atomic explosion of once having paid attention to one of those particles." He further suggests that one key to understanding the radical changes in poetics that many of his contemporaries have introduced in the postmodern era lies in understanding the "different picture" of nature offered by quantum mechanics:

> And now of course I think we have got a different picture with particle physics, in which happenings are really that form [a field of time], I think expanded beyond the field I was picturing in which there could even be a path; because they dont (sic) even see these pathways there and think of it as events. Some guy who got the Nobel prize this year . . . is convinced that particles are individuals; this means that you don't have 32 particles. Every event you see in the particle level is an individual event, and that just blasts wide open the picture even of the field I guess, so what do we do then in language, and why does language change, why does our concept of a form of a poem change?[7]

Duncan's emphasis on poetic form toward the end of this passage suggests that the question of *how* poetry and physics might be connected in esthetic terms is a significant one: "Science is always advancing new pictures of what the universe is . . . When you really had a massive conversion [i.e., a paradigm shift in science] . . . you have a conversion of form [in poetry as well as in physics] entirely."[8]

Critics have noted Duncan's insistence on the importance of quantum physics as both an esthetic and a hermeneutical tool in the crafting and interpretation of verse. Mark Andrew Johnson observes that an understanding of Heisenberg matrices is required for a full comprehension of Duncan's own matrices of words in his 1968 volume *Bending the Bow*. Duncan's method "sends the reader to nuclear physics," Johnson argues, "for it evokes the matrices with which field physicists represent three-dimensional electron patterns in a two-dimensional mathematical grid."[9] Moreover, Johnson suggests that the direct influence of physics on Duncan's thinking is so pervasive that one-to-one linkages between Duncan and a particular physicist aren't necessary: "Duncan's method here [*The Fire: Passages 13*"] opens the poem with an asyntactic structure, charged with energy and meaning in infinite combinations, regardless of Duncan's awareness of Pauli or Heisenberg."[10] Johnson also claims that the renowned particle physicist Murray Gell-Mann's

> breakthrough in particle physics helped expand [Duncan's] notion of the universe and consequently of poetry . . . Gell-Mann first announced his theory in 1964, the year of this "Passage." Whether Duncan knew it then or not, the interest in physics is there, and the multiple ramifications of the matrix that opens and strongly closes this poem are no less rich.[11]

Duncan wouldn't always seek as models for poetic form the elegant mathematical symmetries or matrices of physicists like Murray Gell-Mann. By keeping up with the rapidly changing field of quantum mechanics, he could share with Bowering and Hogg in 1977 his interest in a new theory which claimed that "every event you see at the particle level is an individual event." And yet the work of both Duncan and Gell-Mann demonstrates the ability of poet and physicist to borrow from each other in their struggles to find a language (for Gell-Mann, *quarks*, a literary word; for Duncan, *particles*, a scientific term) to describe states of energy and states of being. The physicist, of course, is more at home in the language of mathematics, even as Duncan's topos is verse; nonetheless, the singular importance of the principles of both biophysics and quantum physics for Duncan's poetics is clear and compelling.

In "Towards an Open Universe," Duncan mentions Erwin Schrödinger five times and quotes him three times. Indeed, of the physicists with whom Duncan appears to be familiar, the one to whom he returns most often in conversation and in writing is Schrödinger. Here I'll argue that, although Duncan does not mention it directly, the Schrödinger wave function represents as unique and indispensable a hermeneutical tool as Schrödinger's biophysics for a full understanding of Duncan's self-referential verse.

According to Ian W. Reid, "Duncan consistently rejects the notion that the language of poetry is instrumental, merely denoting realities external to itself. For him it is primarily self-referential."[12] For Duncan, as his friend and occasional mentor Jack Spicer remarked, "the poem begins to mirror itself."[13] Before investigating ways in which Schrödinger's wave function may be applied as a tool for uncoding Duncan's self-referential language, however, it's necessary to describe the mechanics of the wave function itself.

The Schrödinger wave function in physics is a mathematical description of a set of possibilities which pertains to a given quantum system. Position and momentum of elementary particles represent two such possibilities. To measure the position, say, of a particle, the physicist must, as Schrödinger says, "disentangle" the position from the momentum; this is the only way to "gather further information" or measure the system.[14] What's fascinating about wave function dynamics from the angle of Robert Duncan's physics-oriented poetics is that the act of disentangling a quantum system means much more than observing it: the physicist *interacts* with the system as he measures it. He cannot, in other words, objectively measure the system.

In a quantum context, each possibility which is governed by the wave function is as authentic as the next possibility until the system is measured— until, that is, an observer engages with the system. At that moment a hump in the wave function collapses: i.e., one possibility collapses, while the other is actualized by the act of observation. If no observer measures the system, then, as the physicist Gary Zukav argues, the universe exists as a "profusion of possibilities."[15] The best-known model of wave function dynamics is "Schrödinger's cat," the thought experiment in which a cat in a box lives or dies depending on whether a device containing poison gas is triggered by the radioactive decay of an atom whose half-life is one hour. This means that one hour after the cat was placed in the box, there's a 50-50 chance that the cat is alive. Zukav explains the key role played by human observers in the cat's fate:

> The Copenhagen Interpretation of quantum mechanics says that the cat is *in a kind of limbo* represented by a wave function which contains the possibility that the cat is dead and also the possibility that the cat is alive. When we look in the box, and not before, one of these possibilities actualizes and the other vanishes. This is known as the collapse of the wave function because the hump in the wave function representing the possibility that did not occur, collapses. It is necessary to look into the box before either possibility can occur. Until then, there is only a wave function.[16]

If the wave function is a set of possibilities, *all of which are real,* then Schrödinger's cat is literally both alive and dead at the same time until the box is opened—a situation which classical physics and philosophy would find absurd. In short, Schrödinger's cat needs the observer in order for its measurable destiny to be actualized. As Zukav concludes, "We are actualizing the universe. Since we are part of the universe, that makes the universe (and us) self-actualizing."[17] In what ways can Schrödinger's wave function be applied to a poetic text in as precise a manner as the conventional literary categories of theme, imagery, meter or stanzaic structure?

"Spelling," from *Bending the Bow,* is a poem that, like Schrödinger's cat, carries on a dual existence in the mind of the reader/observer. It dismantles its own sounds and spellings in what first appears to be a dry-as-dust exercise in phonetics—"/k/ examples: **kan, kind, kreep, klime, kween, skin**, skratch, thikker, brakken, siks, kase, kure, kreem, klame, kwarter, skwire, konker, distinkt, **eksamplz**".[18] In fact these sound-spellings constitute what in "Towards an Open

Universe" Duncan calls a dance to describe the interrelationships between human consciousness and matter itself. Duncan introduces "Spelling" with a stage direction:

> . . . passages in bold face and in Greek letters should be written on a blackboard as they arise in the course of the dance of words and phrasings that is also the earnest mimesis of a classroom exposition, keeping in the motion of the writing as in the sound of the reading the felt beat in which the articulations of the time of the poem dance. . . .[19]

Duncan's directions for the reading of the poem indicate that "Spelling" is meant to be a performance, not merely a poem to be read passively. But how does one read such a poem? And what is the relationship between the performance and the thing to be performed? Put another way, what is the relationship between form and content in "Spelling"? One usually thinks of the content of a dance as the program written and choreographed for the dancer, and thus interpreted by the dancer. Dance, of course, is a favorite metaphor of poets and physicists alike to describe the relationships between the poet or the physicist—or anyone—and the system he is entering, whether it happens to be language or quantum phenomena. When W.B. Yeats asks his famous rhetorical question at the end of "Among School Children," "O body swayed to music, O brightening glance / How can we know the dancer from the dance?", the dance represents Plato's "ghostly paradigm of things," and the dancer is the flesh-and-blood human being who seeks a balance between matter and spirit.[20] In physics, the question, "How can we know the dancer from the dance?" is no less perplexing:

> I think it would be misleading to call particles the entities involved in the most primitive events of the theory (quantum topology) because they don't move in space and time, they don't carry mass, they don't have charge, they don't have energy in the usual sense of the word.

32

QUESTION: So what is it that makes events at that level?
ANSWER: Who are the dancers and who are the dance? They have
no attributes other than the dance.
QUESTION: What is 'they'?[21]

Robert Duncan is clearly aware of the significance of the dancer/dance
conundrum to both physicist and poet. When he observes in the 1977 interview with
Bowering and Hogg that particle physicists "dont (sic) even see these pathways . . .
and think of it as events," he registers his affinity for the same fundamental paradox
which is rooted in the physicist's question concerning particles, "What is 'they?' "
A decade earlier, in the dance of "Spelling," "events," or "particles" (Duncan's
favorite metaphor for syllables in the sixties) manifest themselves as X-rays of the
poem's own language: "A K E, the verb being of the order of *take, shake, make* the
substantive pronounced /eis/ or "H," until 1700."[22] However, these pauses
themselves constitute part of the field, or poem, which they are busy X-raying.

Michael Davidson has termed these philological asides in Duncan's poems
"lexical inserts." He claims correctly that Duncan is not alone among contemporary
poets in searching out etymologies "in order to provide a gloss on a word or phrase,
the etymology being included as part of the poem itself."[23] In a discussion of
Duncan's poem "At the Loom" *(Passages* 2), Davidson suggests that the insert
"serves both to return a certain materiality to the word (the warp as a dart or arrow,
the shuttle as a door or flood-gate) and to illustrate the 'loom of language' that is the
poem's subject."[24] For Davidson, lexical inserts "represent a desire to validate or
authenticate the present moment by an appeal to the past—a past not lost in time but
one that exists in language still very much alive."[25]

Davidson is correct to focus on philology as subject matter in Duncan's verse
and in the verse of poets like Charles Olson and Philip Whalen; nevertheless, a
strictly philological approach to Duncan glosses over two key areas of hermeneutical

inquiry, and is thus limited as a tool for uncoding his self-referential poetics. First, a philological hermeneutics emphasizes the thematic *why* of the presence of lexical inserts in poetry—i.e., it's (literally) logocentered. What remains to be uncoded is the *how,* the inner workings of Duncan's lexical scheme. Second, the philological approach ignores the central role of the reader that the poem clearly foregrounds. The Schrödinger wave function provides the necessary key to open up for study both these hidden hermeneutical agendas in Duncan's poetry.

In "Spelling," for instance, Duncan's method is both ontological and esthetic: he continually forces the reader to make a decision, in every line of the poem, as to what the poem *is,* as opposed to what the poem *says.* The poem challenges and perplexes the reader with precisely the same knotty questions concerning the matter of language that perplex the physicists in the dialogue above concerning the language of matter. For the question persists in "Spelling": Is there a message (a dancer) between the lines of self-referentiality (the dance)? Is the poem a *pas de deux* between the meaning of its language and the X-rays of its language? Is the poem dancer or dance? Are the dance and dancer one?

In fact, Duncan appears to want "Spelling" to be both dancer and dance. In the closing lines, he makes a neat phonetic match between an aside, an intertextual X-ray of another literary work, and the speaker's voice, by quoting from Conan Doyle's *The Great Shadow:*

> "I wish your eyes would always flash like that, for
> it looks so nice and manly."
> It looks so nicen manly.[26]

The reader hears the same sounds from the quoted passage by Conan Doyle and the speaker of "Spelling." Yet the different spellings of *nice and* and *nicen* create a dissonance, a duality, which ends the poem on an appropriately paradoxical note. To the ear, the words are the same; to the eye, they are different. "Nice and" and "nicen" both function as humps in the wave function of Duncan's language. Thus, in "Spelling," Duncan appears to have accomplished the feat of transmuting a scientific structural model into an esthetic one.

Wave function hermeneutics apply elsewhere in *Bending the Bow*. The title of "At the Loom *(Passages 2)*" reveals the theme of the poem: the process of making a poem. Of course there's nothing new in English or American literature about poetry as subject matter for poetry. And "At the Loom" begins in a conventional way, talking about the poetical process:

> . . . my mind a shuttle among
> set strings of the music
> lets a weft of dream grow in the day time,
> an increment of associations,
> luminous soft threads,
> the thrown glamour, crossing and recrossing,
> the twisted sinews underlying the work.[27]

As is the case in "Spelling," however, in the last line the conventional thematic regime of making a poem as the subject of the poem is replaced by a new metapoetics of form that recalls the self-referential narrative poetics of metafictionists like John Barth and Robert Coover. The reader is obliged to ask, exactly what are the twisted sinews underlying the work?

Even as "At the Loom" begins to call attention to itself as a weaving, even as the lyric weaves a pattern, Duncan suddenly begins to unravel the poem in order to scrutinize what the poem is made of:

> Let there be the clack of the shuttle flying
> > forward and back,
> > > forward and
> > > > back,
> warp, *wearp, varp: "cast of a net, a laying of eggs"*
> > from *warp—"to throw"*
> the threads twisted for strength
> > that can be a warp of the will. . . . [28]

Duncan makes his verbs do double duty by performing as verbs and also by calling attention (as verbs) to their very performance (as verbs). Even as the verb *warp* helps Duncan to weave the poem, suddenly *warp* begins to unravel, spinning etymological threads through the poem. The reader is immediately jarred loose from any conventional logocentered assumptions about what a poem is. Is the sudden etymology of *warp* an insert or a pause in the poem, while the rest of the poem gazes at itself as it were ("The poem begins to mirror itself") in the mirror of its own language? But, of course, the mirror of language also constitutes the poem.

Insofar as Duncan reveals an ancillary interest in teasing out, thread by thread, the origins of the artistic impulse itself, the theme of "At the Loom"—like that of "Spelling"—is consistent with its wave function. The poem also mirrors itself in the noun "shuttle":

> And the shuttle carrying the woof I find
> > was *skutill "harpoon"*—a dart, an arrow,
> > > or a little ship
> > *navicula weberschif,*
>
> crossing and recrossing from shore to shore—
> > prehistoric *skutil skut*—
> > "A bolt, a bar, as of a door"
> > "a flood-gate"[29]

The etymology of *warp* reveals the infinitive *to throw*; the etymology of *shuttle* reveals the noun *harpoon*; thus Duncan reveals a dark, perhaps even primordial, side to the eternal oppositions between warp and woof. Equally important, Duncan's metapoetics in "At the Loom" present a weaving that unravels its warp and woof, so that the unraveling is the weaving—i.e., is the poem. Moreover, the reader is asked to consider whether or not the two impulses represented by the poem—the creative drive in the poet and the destructive drive in the warrior—also represent a weaving/ unraveling continuum of humps in the poem's thematic wave function:

> . . . the hand trained to the bow,
>   the man's frame
> withstanding, each side
> facing its foe for the sake of
>   the alliance,
> allegiance, the legion, that the
>   vow that makes a nation
> one body not be broken[30]

"At the Loom," therefore, presents the reader with a double wave function: it X-rays its own language, investigating what the language is even as we recognize that the process of investigating what the language *is*, is what the language *does*. And the poem also meshes its self-referential poetics with its theme, for "At the Loom" is concerned with the simultaneous human impulses to make poetry and to make war, impulses "dreadful and surmounting dread," yet "luminous" at the same time. The reader collapses the wave function of one thematic category by focusing on the other, and by approaching the poem either esthetically—exploring how it means—or ontologically—examining what it is. The choices the reader makes, however, can never subsume or define the poem either thematically *or* technically, because Duncan insists on the luminosity of the system *as a whole*, a luminosity which shimmers in the etymological threads of "At the Loom": the simultaneous weaving and unravelling of warp and woof.

In "The Collage *(Passages 6)*," Duncan chooses another conventional metaphor—architecture—for making the poem:

>   paste-up the city
>   we build up of blocks the
>   alpha beta and this
>   is gamma so placed
>   as Henry Miller once named the Delta
>   his vehicle, and
>   Her zone, Her parvis
>   is language Pythagoras knew,
>   leading to the life-door, the cunt . . .[31]

Like "Spelling" and "At the Loom," "The Collage" quickly abandons convention—the architectural building blocks of language as described above—and becomes unabashedly self-referential: " . . . beyond how wet the air will/come and carry these vowels?/these dentals, labials . . ."[32] "The Collage" also interrupts itself, so that the speaker can make a critical commentary on the poem in progress: "[I mean to force up emblems again into these passages of a poetry, passages made conglomerate, the pyramid that dense, a mountain, immovable; cut ways in it then and trick the walls with images establishing space and time for more than the maker knows he acknowledges . . .]."[33] The speaker appears to stop the poem and announce his intentions: "I mean to force up emblems [among them Greek letters] again into these passages of a poetry . . ."; then, directly following the interregnum, the poem resumes:

>   This way below is the way above,
>   the mouth of the cave or temple growing moist
>   shining,   to allow   the neophyte
>   full entrance . . .[34]

The sexual theme of the poem appears to take over from the critical commentary about the images attached to the sexual theme. But again Duncan has raised a fundamental question. What, precisely, constitutes the poem? Does the poem include the commentary? Or is the commentary meant to be read as separate from the poem? If so, then why does Duncan place it in the *middle* of the poem, as opposed to, say, having placed the stage directions for the reading of "Spelling" at the beginning of that poem? And who is the maker alluded to at the end of the commentary? Are we to understand that there are two speakers in "The Collage," or two voices, a speaker and a maker? These questions may be answered in different ways, but what's clear is that Duncan has performed a typically postmodernist sleight-of-hand by making the boundary between criticism and literature fuzzy. We aren't quite sure if the "I" of the commentary ("I mean to force up . . .") is the same "I" of the rest of the poem, or if one can make such a distinction at all.

In "Towards an Open Universe," Duncan insists that always the "inner structure of the universe has the [immediate] event to be recognized."[35] By *immediate event* Duncan indicates what is for him the key connection between the epistemes of quantum physics and aperiodic verse: both systems challenge the interpretive strategies of human beings with what Milec Capek in *The Philosophical Impact of Contemporary Physics* calls "the evidence of our immediate experience." Capek and Duncan share the quantum assumption that "every present event is undoubtedly caused, though not necessitated by its own past. For as long as it is not yet present, its specific character remains uncertain."[36] For Duncan, what the physicist Capek calls "the hesitation of reality" includes more than a set of interpretive strategies, represented by imagery, assonance, rhythm, etc., designed to uncode the meanings of the lyric.[37] In Duncan's view, the hesitation of reality is the subject matter of the poem.

Where, then, do poet and physicist part company? Once the consciousness of the observer comes into play, Schrödinger's cat can only be *experienced* as alive or dead; the reader of a poem, on the other hand, can entertain several manifestations of language in his mind, consciously and unconsciously, at the same time. Of course the differences between reading a poem and observing the nature of physical reality are elemental and profound: they are rooted in even broader distinctions between epistemology—categories of knowledge—and ontology—modes of being. Nevertheless, in re-shaping a physicist's ideas into bold new configurations of a poet's esthetics, Robert Duncan demonstrates that the invitation to the dance of the syllables and stanzas of open form may be extended by physicist and poet alike.

———————

NOTES

1.   Robert Duncan *(1919-1988)* was co-leader with Jack Spicer of the so-called Berkeley Poetry Renaissance of the late forties and early fifties. Like Charles Olson and many of his West Coast contemporaries, Duncan was an avid practitioner of open form or field poetics. Duncan was influenced by a wide range of poets and writers, from St. John of the Cross and Apollinaire to Virginia Woolf and Ezra Pound. Duncan's publications over a 40-year career include the volumes *Heavenly City, Earthly City, Caesar's Gate: Poems 1949-1950, The Opening of the Field, Roots and Branches, The Years as Catches, Tribunals: Passages 31-35,* and *An Ode and Arcadia* (with Jack Spicer).

—from *Pages from a Notebook*:

Croce thinks with Vico that poetry is a kind of thot [sic] primitive to science, and that the imagination creates in poetry an inarticulate ground from which particulars and exactitudes are distinguished. Only ideas of poetry develop from the ideas of poetry. For the poet, science seems like poetry itself a primitive conceiving of things.

2.   Robert Duncan, "Towards an Open Universe," in *The Poetics of the New American Poetry*, ed. Donald Allen and Warren Tallman (New York: Grove Press, 1973), p. 224.

3.   *Ibid.*, p. 214.

4.   *Ibid.*, p. 214.

5.   David Bohm, *Wholeness and the Implicate Order* (London: Routledge and Kegan Paul, 1980), p. 194.

6.   Sherman Paul, *The Lost America of Love: Rereading Robert Creeley, Edward Dorn, and Robert Duncan* (Baton Rouge: Louisiana State University Press, 1981), pp. 243-44.

7.   George Bowering and Robert Hogg, *Robert Duncan: An Interview* (Toronto: Coach House Press, 1971), n.p.

8.   Mark Andrew Johnson, *Robert Duncan* (Boston: Twayne Publishers, 1988).

9.   Johnson, *Robert Duncan*, p. 110.

10.   *Ibid.*, p. 110.

11.   *Ibid.*, p. 110.

12.   Ian W. Reid, "The Plural Text: 'Passages,'" in *Robert Duncan: Scales of the Marvelous*, ed. Robert J. Berthoff and Ian W. Reid (New York: New Directions, 1979), p. 175.

13.   Jack Spicer, *The Collected Books of Jack Spicer*, ed. Robin Blaser (Los Angeles: Black Sparrow Press, 1975), p. 265.

14.   Erwin Schrödinger, "Discussions of Probability Relations Between Squared Systems," *Cambridge Philosophical Society Proceedings* 31 (1935): 555.

15.   Gary Zukav, *The Dancing Wu Li Masters: An Overview of the New Physics* (New York: Bantam Books, 1979), p. 79.

16.   *Ibid.*, p. 79.

17.   *Ibid.*, p. 86.

18.   Robert Duncan, *Bending the Bow* (New York: New Directions, 1968), p. 49.

19.   *Ibid*, p. 48.

20.   William Butler Yeats, "Among School Children," in *Selected Poems and Two Plays of William Butler Yeats*, ed. M. L. Rosenthal (New York: Collier Books, 1966), p. 117.

21.   Zukav, *The Dancing Wu Li Masters*, p. 317.

22.   Duncan, *Bending the Bow*, p. 49.

23.   Michael Davidson, " 'From the Latin *speculum*': the Modern Poet as Philologist," *Contemporary Literature* 28 (Summer 1987): 187.

24.   *Ibid.*, p. 188.

25.   *Ibid.*, p. 189.

26.   Duncan, *Bending the Bow*, p. 50.

27.   *Ibid.*, p. 11.

28.   *Ibid.*, p. 12.

29.   *Ibid.*, p. 12.

30.   *Ibid.*, p. 12.

31.   *Ibid.*, p. 19.

32.   *Ibid.*, p. 19.

33.   *Ibid.*, p. 19.

34.   *Ibid.*, p. 19.

35.   Duncan, "Towards an Open Universe," p. 224.

36.   Milic Capek, *The Philosophical Impact of Contemporary Physics* (New York: Van Rinehold Nostrand Company, 1961), p. 340.

37.   *Ibid.*, p. 340.

Jack Spicer's Quantum Poetics

I

R eaders of Jack Spicer's[1] poetry occasionally encounter Einsteinian cosmology head on: "Distance, Einstein said, goes around in circles. This/Is the opposite of a party or a social gathering."[2] Elsewhere, on a grimmer note, Spicer asks his readers to enter "The unstable universe," which "has distance but not much else."[3] It's a lonely universe mirrored in "The tidal swell" of Stinson Beach, which itself is constituted of "Particle and wave/Wave and particle/Distances."[4] The appearance of quanta in Spicer's work isn't merely thematic: the chiasmus—the speaker crosses over from particle and wave to wave and particle—mirrors the way electrons "cross over" from wave to particle, depending on how they are observed by physicists. This is elementary quantum physics as expressed by an elementary literary device, the chiasmus. But in a poem from the "Morphemics" section of his volume, *Language*, Spicer adds a complex feature to the equation:

> Lew, you and I know how love and death matter
> Matter as wave and particle—twins
> At the same business.[5]

The syntactical ambiguity between the first and second lines, and the pun on "matter" itself, are doubly significant. The constituents of matter (wave and particle) and the classic constituents of poetry (love and death) form one linguistic system.[6] Wave and particle is not a metaphor for love and death, nor is love and death a metaphor for wave and particle. The parallel is clearly thematic, but as "matter/Matter," both systems also represent two sides of the same linguistic coin: it's the syntax that erases conventional boundaries between states of energy/matter (wave and particle) and states of being/nonbeing (love and death).

The Newtonian laws of motion that pertain to the macrocosm, or the world of the everyday where people throw balls in the air and expect them to come down again, don't always apply to the world of the quantum. As a professional linguist, Jack Spicer was keenly aware that everyday language is in strict fealty to Newton's everyday cosmos: the laws of language (subject-verb-object) mirror the laws of nature (John throws the ball to Robert). But language may *also* disobey Newtonian laws—in syntax, grammar, metaphor—even as quanta do. Spicer observes that "We make up a different language for poetry/And for the heart—ungrammatical."[7] Even the "language of the heart"—everyday words and sentences which people speak to each other—fails when we "cannot quite make the sounds of love/The language/Has so misshaped them."[8]

Quantum poetics[9] and quantum physics share another epistemological feature: both systems are dedicated to tearing down boundaries that the human mind has artificially imposed upon matter and language. According to the physicist J.M. Jauch, modern scientists routinely question the boundary between macrocosm and microcosm:

> . . . we maintain that all our macroscopic bodies of classical physics are composed of atoms and elementary particles held together by forces of various kinds. There must therefore exist a boundary where the classical description ceases to have validity and the quantum properties become dominant. Now nobody knows the exact position of the boundary. Most people would agree that the experimental apparatus with which we execute the experiments and the computers with which we evaluate the data are on the classical side, and therefore behave according to the laws of classical physics. But between this input and output there is a system, like the photons . . . which behaves quite differently from any classical system that we know. Thus, by setting a boundary somewhere, on one side

of which things are classical and on the other side quantal, we cause almost insoluble problems of fundamental importance.[10]

Thus, the most hallowed boundary of all, the line between the Newtonian world of classical mechanics and the quantum realm, may not exist—at least in configurations that make sense to us at present.

Jack Spicer is similarly suspicious of the artificial boundaries created by language:

Let us tie the strings on this bit of reality.
Graphemes. One wax now plastic, showing the ends. Like a
        red light.
One feels or sees limits.
They are warning graphemes but also meaning graphemes
        because without the marked ends of the shoelace or the
        traffic signal one would not know how to tie a shoe or cross
        a street—which is like making a sentence.[11]

"Let them snarl at you," the speaker says of graphemes, "and you snarl back at them." The act of snarling is the act of writing the poem that snarls at its own graphemes. "Crossing a street against the light . . . is all right," the speaker goes on, "Freedom in fact."[12] As we'll see, however, linguistic freedom is not without its significant risks.

Spicer's radical suspicions of linguistic boundaries even extend to the human imagination itself and its interrelationships with the Newtonian cosmos. Spicer describes an Orphic stance for the poet in the world.

. . . from what I've seen . . . there's no question that objective events can be caused in order for poems to be written. Robin [Blaser] in "The Moth Poems" had moths just coming in the wildest places, something where the odds would be about a million to one of the

46

moths being just exactly in the place that he wanted the poems written, but I was there a couple of times when it happened. And I think that it is certainly possible that the objective universe can be affected by the poet. I mean—you recall Orpheus made the trees and stones dance, and so forth—and this is something which is in almost all primitive cultures, and it, I think, has some definite basis to it.[13]

Although Spicer invokes Greek myth in order to suggest that the poetical imagination and the so-called objective world may not constitute two separate systems, one modern quantum physicist believes that such a reciprocal metasystem is real, not "mythological." *In Wholeness and the Implicate Order*, David Bohm theorizes that

the body enfolds not only the mind but also in some sense the entire material universe . . . both through the senses and through the fact that the constituent atoms of the body are actually structures that are enfolded in principle throughout all space.[14]

Bohm points out that even in commonsensical everyday existence, reciprocity between the crude categories of mind and matter is hardly a rare occurrence:

. . . we know it to be a fact that the physical state can affect the content of consciousness in many ways (the simplest case is that we can become conscious of neural excitations as sensations). Vice versa, we know that the content of consciousness can affect the physical state (*e.g.*, from a conscious intention nerves may be excited, muscles may move, the heartbeat change, along with alterations of glandular activity, blood chemistry, etc.).[15]

For both Spicer, the poet, and Bohm, the physicist, "the psyche," as Carl Jung has written, "cannot be localized in space or . . . space is relative to the psyche." Jung elaborates:

Synchronistic phenomena prove the simultaneous occurrence of meaningful equivalences in heterogeneous, causally unrelated processes; in other words, they prove that a content perceived by an observer can, at the same time, be represented by an outside event, without any causal connection.[16]

In a whimsical poem from the "Intermissions" section of *Language*, Spicer suggests that the poet also participates in Jungian acausality:

> Where is the poet? A-keeping the sheep
> A-keeping the celestial movement of the spheres in a long,
>   boring procession
> A-center of gravity
> A-(while the earthquakes of happiness go on inside and outside
>   his body and the stars in their courses stop to notice)
> Sleep.[17]

Perhaps like William Blake, who hated Newtonian cosmology, and who felt that "The stars were in the heavens because man's imagination saw them there,"[18] Jack Spicer takes seriously the possibility that the physical universe, and man's perception of it, don't necessarily constitute two separate and distinct systems.

In epistemological sync with both the latter-day thinkers David Bohm and Carl Jung, Jack Spicer seeks to restructure the devices of poetry in order to pay proper tribute in language to such a universe. Perhaps the most interesting feature of Spicer's quantum poetics is the deconstructions of metaphor which appear in his later work.

48

II

Of all poetical conventions, the metaphor is particularly user-friendly in a Newtonian universe, where distinctions between here/there and either/or are taken for granted. Indeed, the two working parts of a classic metaphor, tenor and vehicle, reinforce epistemological distinctions between real and fanciful, between worldly cheeks and imaginary apples in the metaphor "apple cheeks," for instance. To the poet who takes the Newtonian universe for granted, real apples Scotch-taped to real cheeks would be an absurd literalization. To the Newtonian scientist, imaginary apples are pretty in poetry, but only the cheeks are real. These distinctions, which assume that linguistic systems must slavishly obey the laws of the macrocosm, extend to the taboo that we must never mix our metaphors.

The world of the quantum, however, presents the observer with very different laws. Subatomic particles simply don't behave like objects in Newtonian space. Physicists perceive that the difficulties of interpretation which quanta present them with aren't merely mathematical; they're *linguistic* as well. As Werner Heisenberg has observed, "All the words or concepts we use to describe ordinary physical objects, such as position, velocity, color, size, and so on, become indefinite and problematic if we try to use them on elementary particles."[19] The difficulty, however, cannot simply be pinned down to words alone. Some physicists wonder whether conventional distinctions between "real" and "unreal"—the heart of the matter of metaphor—always apply to the microcosm, where the question "Are quanta real?" is taken with the utmost seriousness.[20]

Jack Spicer takes the same aggressive, questioning stance toward the metaphors of poetry. The following poem from *Language* provides a good example of the poet's guerrilla strategy against metaphor:

Sporting Life
The trouble with comparing a poet with a radio is that radios
    don't develop scar-tissue. The tubes burn out, or with a
    transistor, which most souls are, the battery or diagram
    burns out replaceable or not replaceable, but not like that
    punchdrunk fighter in the bar. The poet
Takes too many messages. The right to the ear that floored him
    in New Jersey. The right to say that he stood six rounds with
    a champion.
Then they sell beer or go on sporting commissions, or, if the
    scar tissue is too heavy, demonstrate in a bar where the
    invisible champions might not have hit him. Too many of
    them.
The poet is a radio. The poet is a liar. The poet is a counter-
    punching radio.
And those messages (God would not damn them) do not even
    know they are champions.[21]

Like a Cubist painting, "Sporting Life" offers the spectator/reader a familiar image, the neoclassical metaphor of the poet as transmitter, updated as a radio. Then, as in Cubism, the poem proceeds to tear its subject matter to pieces—in the case of "Sporting Life," the subject matter includes metaphors for the poet and the speaker's avowed skepticism of those metaphors.

In "Sporting Life," Spicer's deconstructions of metaphor occur on three levels. First, the poet plants a seed of doubt in the reader's mind by pointing out a flaw in the analogy between poet and radio which extends throughout the poem: "radios don't develop scar tissue." Second, the poet further undercuts the metaphor by breaking the rules of metaphor and mixing poet as radio with poet as fighter: "The poet is a counterpunching radio." Finally, the speaker shatters *both* metaphors by telling the reader, "The poet is a liar." What the poet is, in other words, can only be expressed metaphorically, and thus falsely. Only the messages which come from an outside source unknown to the poet ("God would not damn them") are real. Spicer's version of Epimenides' Cretan paradox, "The poet is a liar," forces the reader into a thicket of impossible questions, among them: Is the poet (the speaker) a liar who is telling the truth through metaphor? Or is he a trustworthy speaker who is lying through metaphor? If these questions don't make sense, neither do conventional metaphors, which, according to the metaphorical poet, always allow some awful truth ("scar tissue") to escape. For Spicer, these deconstructions of metaphor aren't clever apparatuses that mirror the content of the poem; the deconstructions *are* the content of the poem.

Spicer's attacks on metaphor can be obscene:

> For you I would build a whole new universe around myself.
>   This isn't shit it is poetry. Shit
> Enters into it only as an image.[22]

Or:

> In my heart, as Verlaine said, I can hear the little sound of it
>   raining
> Not an Indian sign. But real unfucking rain.[23]

More often, the attacks are poignant:

> Sandy growls like a wolf. The space between him and his image
>   is greater than the space between me and my image.
> Throw him a honey-cake. Hell has been proved to be a series of
>   image.
> Death is a dog and Little Orphan Annie
> My own Eurydice. Going into hell so many times tears it
> Which explains poetry.[24]

Here, Spicer uses two familiar comic strip characters to suggest that the "series of image" which "Hell has been proved to be" is a flat-out lie. Death and Hell are appallingly *un*metaphorical; they're all too real to the speaker who has gone "into hell so many times." Thus, the poem punches through the pasteboard masks of its own metaphors: Sandy who growls like a wolf becomes Cerberus; Little Orphan Annie becomes Eurydice; both comic strip characters are always a step (a vehicle) away from the real. Because human beings don't suffer metaphorically , the "space" between them and their images is "greater" than the poet's. Human suffering "explains poetry," and also explains the speaker's radical suspicions of the very metaphors that appear in his own poetry.

Spicer's deconstructions of metaphor are occasionally playful, as in the erotic baseball poems from *Book of Magazine Verse*:

> I would like to beat my hands around your heart.
> You are a young pitcher but you throw fast curve-balls, slow
>   fast-balls, change-ups that at the last moment don't change.
>   Junk
> The pitchers who are my age call it. And regret every forty
>   years of their life when they have to use them.[25]

The speaker concludes,

>   . . . Off seasons
> I often thought of praying to Him but could not stand the
>   thought of that big, white, round omnipotent bastard.
> Yet He's there. As the game follows rules He makes them.
> I know
> I was not the only one who felt these things[26]

As opposed to a stereotypical white-bearded patriarch, God is compared to a baseball. What the speaker "could not stand," of course, was the "thought of" God as a metaphor, even though human beings are doomed *always* to think of Him metaphorically. Once the baseball disappears in the last two lines (along with the geometric logic of Newtonian laws of motion), the poem becomes a simple statement of faith *or* of cosmic/comic desperation, depending on how one chooses to interpret the tone of the last line.

III

Spicer draws a parallel between the matter of language and the language of matter in a series of lectures he gave at the Vancouver Poetry Festival in the summer of 1965. He finds degrees of complexity in language analogous to "the most simple particles and the more complicated particles in chemistry-physics."[27] But, as Spicer might have added, the trouble with comparing words with particles, as if the poem were merely a sort of linguistic particle accelerator, is that neither words nor particles develop scar tissue. Put another way, for Spicer deconstruction of language—of metaphor in particular—becomes deconstruction of self. Every metaphor is a mask. So are the poets who make them:

> What I am, I want, asks everything of everyone, is by degrees a ghost.
> Steps down to the first metaphor they invented in the underworld
> (pure and clear like a river) the insight. As a place to step further.[28]

A place to step further means that every tenor in poetry is a mask (a disguised vehicle) for another tenor. That tenor is a mask (a disguised vehicle) for another tenor, and so forth. Similarly, every human being is a mask for a ghost. For Spicer, *ghost* may also be a metaphor for the Other, the hidden voice or shadow that every poet desires to capture in the perfect poem. If the speaker of the poem is by degrees a ghost, then no boundary exists between him and the Other. The speaker may be real (tenor) and the Other may be imaginary (vehicle). *Or the reverse may be true:*

Poetry comes along after the city [of poets] is collected. It recognizes *them* as a metaphor. An unavoidable metaphor. Almost the opposite.[29]

Spicer's view of poetry, which mysteriously comes along after the city is collected, resembles Michel Foucault's description of the Other, or the ideal *unthought*, which always escapes human attempts to grasp it:

> Man and the unthought are, at the archaeological level, contemporaries. Man has not been able to describe himself as a configuration in the episteme without thought at the same time discovering, both in itself and outside itself, at its borders yet also in its very warp and woof, an element of darkness, an apparently inert density in which it is embedded, an unthought which it contains entirely, yet in which it is also caught. The unthought (whatever name we give it) is not lodged in man like a shriveled-up nature or a stratified history; it is, in relation to man, the Other: the Other that is not only a brother but a twin, born, not of man, but beside him and at the same time, in an identical newness, in an unavoidable duality.[30]

When Spicer describes as an unavoidable metaphor the relationship between the poet and the ghost of the poem—i.e., the perfect voice which he seeks (in vain) to make his own—he recalls Foucault's unavoidable duality. Both men suggest that, in the mysterious symbiosis between human and Other, the attraction is mutual. For Spicer, poetry becomes

> . . . A silver wire which reaches from the end of the beautiful as if elsewhere. A metaphor. Metaphors are not for humans.
>
> The wires dance in the wind of the noise our poems make.
> The noise without an audience. Because the poems were written for ghosts.

> The ghosts the poems were written for are the ghosts of the poems.
> We have it second-hand. They cannot hear the noise they have been making.
>
> Yet it is not a simple process like a mirror or a radio. They try to give
> us circuits to see them, to hear them. Teaching an audience.[31]

The circuits represent the poet's desire to write the perfect poem. Without that desire, the ghosts disappear from the poem. The poet is left with mere words, that, as Spicer says elsewhere, "are what sticks to the real . . . They are what we hold on with, nothing else. They are as valuable in themselves as rope with nothing to be tied to."[32]

The deconstruction of the poet whose own metaphors turn against him, thus raising the possibility that it is *he* who "was never real,"[33] and the *ghosts* who recognize *him* as a metaphor, takes a terrible toll. At times Spicer is near despair—perhaps beyond despair:

> This is the crab-god shiny and bright
>   who summed by day and wrote by night
>   And lived in the house that Jack built.
> This is the end of it, very dear friend, this
>   is the end of us.[34]

Here, poet and man become one. In the poem (the house), the poet's self (Jack) is as metaphorical as the crab-god which Jack selects as a metaphor for himself. Conversely, Jack may be a metaphor for the crab-god. For the poem reveals that a construction of metaphor is merely a projection of a similarly constructed human self; the infinitely evasive tenor is a verbal projection of the infinitely evasive being of the speaker. Therefore, the deconstructed poet and his deconstructed metaphor end simultaneously as the poem ends: "this/is the end of us." As he lay dying of acute alcoholism at the age of forty, Jack Spicer's last words were, "My vocabulary did this to me."[35]

And yet the poet isn't entirely defeated. The poems remain as testaments to the struggle of every poet to find the perfect poem: a place in language to step no further. Before Jacques Derrida's milestone paper on the Discourses of Human Sciences at Johns Hopkins University in 1966, Jack Spicer had anticipated post-structuralism by insisting that "the perfect poem has an infinitely small vocabulary."[36] What he means, of course, is that the perfect poem cannot be written; it can only be uttered by the still, small intuited voice of the Other, and never in human language. Nevertheless, it's the shadowy presence of the Other (the crab-god) that makes language infinitely beautiful. Two generations after Spicer's untimely death, the speakers of his poems still quarrel with their own metaphors, still quarrel with the ghosts of the poems, who

> . . . won't come through. Nothing comes through. The
> death
> > Of every poem in every line
> > The argument con-
> > > tinues[37]

56

NOTES

1. Jack Spicer *(1925-1965)* came to UC Berkeley from the University of Redlands in the mid-forties. With his friends Robert Duncan and Robin Blaser, Spicer initiated what came to be called the Berkeley Poetry Renaissance. Like William Blake and William Butler Yeats before him, Spicer believed that poetry was dictated by a source outside the poet—what he simply called the Word. The most radically innovative of American poets since the death of Wallace Stevens, Spicer was both mentor and gadfly to many of his peers in the San Francisco Bay area. Ten years after the poet's untimely death in 1965, Black Sparrow Press issued *The Collected Books of Jack Spicer*, edited by Robin Blaser.

    —from *The Heads of the Town Up to the Aether*:

    > "Esstoneish me," the words say that hide behind my alarm
    > clock or my dresser drawer or my pillow. "Etonnez Moi," even
    > the Word says.

    > It is up to us to astonish them and Him. To draw forth
    > answers deep from the caverns of objects or from the Word
    > Himself. Whatever that is.

    > Whatever That is is not a play on words but a play between
    > words, meaning come down to hang on a little cross for a while.
    > In play.

    > And the stony words that are left down with us greet him
    > mutely almost rudely casting their own shadows. For example,
    > the shadow the cross cast.

    > No, now he is the Lowghost when He is pinned down to
    > words.

2. Jack Spicer, *The Collected Books of Jack Spicer*, ed. Robin Blaser (Los Angeles: Black Sparrow Press, 1975), p. 227.

3. *Ibid.*, p. 236.

4. *Ibid.*, p. 277.

5. *Ibid.*, p. 234.

6. The physicist David Bohm proposes what he calls a "rheomode," or a system of radical grammar and syntax, which attempts to bring language more into line with physical reality. For an extended discussion of the rheomode, see Chapter Two of *Wholeness and the Implicate Order* (London: Routledge and Kegan Paul, 1980).

7. Spicer, *The Collected Books of Jack Spicer*, p. 233.

8. *Ibid.*, p. 237.

9.   Susan Strehle's book, *Fiction in the Quantum Universe* (Chapel Hill: University of North Carolina Press, 1992), seeks to apply another version of "quantum poetics" to the postmodern fictions of William Gaddis, John Barth, Margaret Atwood, and others. Strehle defines the quantum poetics of fiction as "actualism," a term she derives from Werner Heisenberg:

> At the subatomic level, [Heisenberg] says, reality is not real,
> but it is active, dynamic, 'actual.' Actualistic fiction expresses,
> then, a literary version of the reality constituted by
> fundamentally new physical theories in the first half of the
> twentieth century. Departing from the stable material reality
> underpinning Newtonian science and realistic fiction,
> actualism abandons and even subverts the narrative
> conventions of realism. (7)

10.   J.M. Jauch, *Are Quanta Real?* (Bloomington: Indiana UP, 1973), pp. 32-33.

11.   Spicer, *The Collected Books of Jack Spicer*, p. 240.

12.   *Ibid.*, p. 240.

13.   Jack Spicer, "From the Vancouver Lectures," *Caterpillar* 12 (July 1970): 206.

14.   Bohm, *Wholeness and the Implicate Order*, p. 209.

15.   *Ibid.*, p. 208.

16.   Carl Jung, *The Portable Jung*, ed. Joseph Campbell (New York: Penguin, 1971), p. 518.

17.   Spicer, *The Collected Books of Jack Spicer*, p. 230.

Elsewhere in this poem Spicer pays tribute to John Donne as another poet who was acutely aware of the scientific discoveries of his time. Spicer begins by quoting Donne:

> "The movement of the earth brings harmes and fears.
> Men wonder what it is and what it meant."
>   Donne
> In the next line
> Contrasts this with "the celestial movement of the spheres."
>   Rhyme soothes . . . (230)

Of the science-minded Donne, Ifor Evans has written,

> John Donne was the first outstanding creative writer to be disturbed by
> the new learning in science and astronomy. The detailed assessment of
> Donne's scientific knowledge has been variously estimated, but in
> reading his work one feels as if an original and creative mind had been
> driven to re-assess his position . . .
>   The new ordering of the universe which science
> seemed to imply led Donne to a new kind of poetry. It was as
> if this awareness led him to be dissatisfied with the old and

> more melodious measures, and the received images.
> (*Literature and Science* [London: Allen & Unwin, Inc., 1954], p. 19)

Much the same could be said of the linguistic relationships between Jack Spicer and the "new science" of twentieth-century quantum mechanics, including Spicer's dissatisfaction with "received image[s]" (see the discussion of Spicer's approach to metaphor below).

18. Alfred Kazin, "Introduction," in *The Portable Blake*, ed. Alfred Kazin (New York: Viking, 1946), p. 4.

19. Qtd. in Gary Zukav, *The Dancing Wu Li Masters: An Overview of the New Physics* (New York: Bantam, Books, 1979), p. 21.

20. The physicist J.M. Jauch devotes his book-length discussion, *Are Quanta Real?,* to this very question.

21. Spicer, *The Collected Books of Jack Spicer*, p. 218.

22. *Ibid.*, p. 239.

23. *Ibid.*, p. 226.

24. *Ibid.*, p. 226.

25. *Ibid.*, p. 256.

26. *Ibid.*, p. 258.

27. Spicer, "From the Vancouver Lectures," p. 210.

28. *Ibid.*, p. 182.

29. *Ibid.*, p. 182.

30. Qtd. in Blaser, "The Practice of Outside," p. 297.

31. Spicer, "From the Vancouver Lectures," p. 170.

32. *Ibid.*, p. 309.

33. *Ibid.*, p. 80.

34. *Ibid.*, p. 233.

35. *Ibid.*, p. 325.

36. *Ibid.*, p. 25.

37. *Ibid.*, p. 171.

Reversible Syntax *vs.* Irreversible Time

K itsch, or the familiarity that breeds complacence if not contempt in critical approaches to the arts, is rooted almost as deeply in the visual aspects of lyric poetry as it is in painting. Complacence, in turn, may tempt the critic to look beyond the obvious in search of meaning, especially where the configurations of everyday experiences in Newtonian time and space are concerned. Thus, in Wordsworth's famous line describing a "host of golden daffodils" dancing in the breeze, the poetics of spacetime is normally accepted by readers as a *donnée*, or a category which is simply there, like a stage set. The equation is: objects (daffodils) + space (breeze) + time (dancing) = image. The flowers dance in space, dance in time, and the grammatical structure of Wordsworth's poetry reflects or expresses the spectacle as choreographed by the poet in the Newtonian macrocosm.

In his attempt to describe a rabbit moving linearly through space, "The hare limp'd trembling through the frozen grass," John Keats adds rhythm to the conventional poetic repertoire of imagery and sound. Here the meter itself limps, demonstrating rhythmically what the words say, so that the hare's progress through the grass can be experienced by the reader on a deeper level than is afforded by imagery alone.

A century after Keats, Robert Frost employs a similar technique of mimetic or programmic rhythms to communicate inertia and then sprightliness in an animal: "My old dog barks backward without getting up./I can remember when he was a pup." The stiffness of the old dog's movement is mirrored in the rare double spondees, "old dog" and "barks back." The elegiac ease of yesteryear's play when the dog was young is mirrored in the scampering accents of "I can remember when

60

he was a pup." Occasionally, modernist writers will break the hallowed rules of grammar and punctuation in order to translate the dynamics of spacetime into language. When James Joyce seeks to convey a young boy's nearly numinous awe of the physical spaces around him, he deliberately eschews the convention of commas separating multiple adjectives: "The high cold empty gloomy rooms liberated me." Here, as Frank O'Connor has noted, the stream of sensations is carefully modulated so that, although Joyce renders them separately, they are fused anyhow in the reader's mind (as they would be for the boy in real life) by the conspicuous blanks left between adjectives where commas should be.[1]

Even as Joyce breaks rules of punctuation, Ernest Hemingway adjusts his language to the demands of Newtonian space by challenging grammatical rules: "I had her watch how Romero took the bull away from a fallen horse with his cape, and how he held him with the cape and turned him, smoothly and suavely, never wasting the bull." In this passage from *The Sun Also Rises*, the ". . . he held him with the cape and turned him . . ." sequence is grammatically faulty because of erroneous reference of personal pronouns; the reader becomes momentarily confused as to who or what the pronouns "he" and "him" refer to, the matador or the bull. But this, of course, is precisely Hemingway's point: at the supreme moment of the bullfight, when the matador and the bull appear to become one, Hemingway's own bold artistic maneuver mimetically blurs the distinction in language between the two so that bull and matador do indeed become one—in language and in the reader's mind.

These latter two prose passages taken from the work of Joyce and Hemingway differ from the first three from Wordsworth, Keats, and Frost, in one important regard: both strongly suggest that English grammatical structures aren't always sufficient to meet the challenges that the rendering of spacetime in language poses for literary imaginations. As for the scientific imagination, Wylie Sypher puts the matter in even bolder terms:

> Using a new kind of Occam's razor, [Ernst] Mach invoked a principle of economy: we must exclude from our accounts of nature every feature not needed to deal with the observations at hand. Such economy would dispense with a Greek logic that had persisted under plausible terms like how, because, in order to, suppose, as a result, although, when, and so on. . . . In brief, the scientist has become aware of the gaps of nature, the conditions that are not amenable to logic. He admits that the hypothesis of comprehensibility breaks down at certain places. . . .[2]

Sypher makes two points worth noting here: first, the marriage of correct or conventional English and the laws of Newtonian physics isn't always a blissful or even a convenient one. Second, scientists need to be aware, even as writers need to be aware, of the potentials and pitfalls of bringing language to bear on spacetime phenomena—of wrestling or pinning nature down to words. In open form poetics, one of these challenges resides in the linguistic applications of nonlinear time.

We know now that the Newtonian paradigm of reversible time represents only part of the cosmic picture. When the physicist David Bohm observes that "more complex orders are possible" than the "abstractions of Newtonian space," he cautions that they must "be described in different ways that cannot generally be reduced to a description in terms of simple sequential orders."[3] Of course, these simple sequential orders include time as well as space, and are commonly expressed verbally in basic Newtonian linguistic structures—i.e., linguistic structures which obey, or reflect, the Newtonian laws of motion.

The classic example of such a Newtonian, or linear, construction is the subject-verb-direct object-indirect object sequence of the sentence, "John throws the ball to Phil." Here, Newtonian dynamics of both action and of reversible time actually govern syntax and structure: the verb acts on the ball as John's arm does so, and the preposition "to" substitutes for space as the ball flies from John to Phil.

Interestingly, although grammarians frown on the weak passive construction, if we reverse the word order to read, "The ball is thrown to Phil by John," the sentence is still grammatically correct. The subjects have changed places in syntactical time; in the latter version, the ball appears first, initiating the lexical action of the sentence. John, who represents the action that begins the sequence, appears last. If we re-write the sentence a third time as, "The ball is thrown by John to Phil," and a fourth time as, "Phil was thrown the ball by John," John appears in the tertiary version *in medias res*, and in the final version changes places with Phil once again.

If we assign the temporal orders A to John, B to the ball, and C to Phil, we see immediately how the sentence is governed by linear, or reversible Newtonian time. In all four versions, the temporal syntactical sequence of John, the ball, and Phil, changes from A — B — C to B — C — A to B — A — C to C — B — A. In like manner, the status of the verb changes from active (John throws) to passive (the ball was thrown). The essential meaning of the sentence, however, remains intact, as does the grammar. In short, the syntactical/grammatical arrow of time in "John throws the ball to Phil" points in two directions, present-future and present-past. The action, however, *remains stubbornly the same*. Thus linear syntactical time is an abstraction, a sort of linguistic despot who rules and refuses to be ruled by his subjects.

A speech from Shakespeare's *The Two Noble Kinsmen*, as interpreted by Charles Olson, illustrates the complexities of linear time dynamics:

> We may outrun
> by violent swiftness that which we run at,
> and lose by overrunning. Know you not
> the fire that mounts the liquor till it run over
> in seeming to augment it wastes it?

Olson focuses on the second line:

> . . . the accents are: 'vi', 'swift', 'that', and 'run', in other words not the five feet blank verse goes by. For a good reason: that the quantity of the syllables (how long it takes to say them) pulls down the accent to a progress of the line along the length of itself, which progress and which quantities the thinking itself, the idea of outrunning, demands. The quantity asserts itself at once with 'by' (long i) and 'violent' (not only long i also, but with two following syllables which, though unaccented, are—the long o and the heavy consonantal syllable 'lent', 3 consonants to 1 vowel—slow to get through). So much so, in fact, that the first breath in the line has here to be taken, even if it is a slight stop before starting to say 'swiftness,' the 't' on the end of 'lent' before the 's' of swiftness requiring the tongue to shift from the upper teethridge (alveolar) off it towards the combined lip and tongue position from which 'sw' may be said.

Then Olson sums up:

> . . . 'by violent' (which is only 1 accent and 4 syllables) already shows forth the weave of accent, quantity, breath which makes prosody the music it is: and here is a very close music, sharp, long and stopped, all in a small space of time, reflecting the truth it is, that this art, when it is at its best, is powerful just because it does obey spacetime.[4]

Shakespeare's poetry is linear in the sense that it obeys Newtonian spacetime in five ways, all of which reflect a threefold tendency toward (a) closure, (b) determinism, and (c) continuity:

1. It relates sound to sense ("The point of Norfolk's thought is to focus the attention on 'violent,' " as Olson observes). Sound-and-sense structures in poetry, like Robert Frost's old dog that barks backward, invite closure because they make language *speak to itself:* sound and sense are thus dovetailed or folded in upon themselves in the line of verse.

2. Shakespeare's meter here is quantitative (not merely blank verse-stressed, as in most of his dramatic poetry). Even though quantitative verse is less predictable than blank verse and its variants, there's still measure in these lines from *The Two Noble Kinsmen*. And measure helps to determine the meaning of dramatic utterance.

3. The lines maintain a consistent tense, or time-measure, in the verb formations: present tense. Thus, continuity with reference to time is achieved.

4. The speech maintains the venerable idiom of coherent and continuous line-formation, a stable left-margin patterning of approximately 10 syllables per line. Closure is also dictated by this classic pattern.

5. The relationship between syntax and meaning is logical, even though the syntax is occasionally inverted ("Know you not . . ."). Note that reversing syntax in the "John throws the ball to Phil" prose model—reversing, that is, the time-sequence of nouns and verbs—didn't change the essential meaning of the sentence either. In Shakespeare's more sophisticated speech, Norfolk makes a declarative statement in grammatical English and illustrates its meaning with a question, an *exemplum*.

In other words, both logic and syntax, not to mention measure, line length, and tense, act as parameters which surround the speech, dictating form and function. Parameter is an important concept for understanding the relationships of linear time to language.

What all these features of linear time have in common is that time is envisioned here as a predictable system, a system in equilibrium. Above all, time is conceived as standing *outside*, or *around,* human experience and language.

But of course the laws of linearity don't always apply to the macrocosm; nor should we expect them to govern the English language with unchallenged sovereignty. When David Bohm suggests that simple sequential orders in Newtonian spacetime don't tell the whole story about macrocosmic systems, he is challenging *continuity*, one of the features of mechanical or linear time:

> Thus, for example, people who know each other well may separate for a long time (as measured by the sequence of moments registered by a clock) and yet they are often able to 'take up from where they left off' as if no time had passed. What we are proposing here is that sequences of moments that 'skip' intervening years are just as allowable forms of time as those which seem continuous.[5]

Like Bohm, Ilya Prigogine eschews Newtonian time-reversible systems in order to posit

> a second time, an internal time quite different from the time that in classical or quantum mechanics simply labels trajectories or wave functions.[6]

Crucial to Prigogine's conception of nonlinear time is its intimate relationship with dissipative structures, such as negentropic bifurcation events in biological systems—i.e., unpredictably complex and creative changes from one state to another. "Dissipative structures," Prigogine claims, "may in turn break the symmetries of spacetime."[7] The resulting "new concepts of time and entropy," Prigogine adds, are not without "consequences . . . which must yet be explored."[8]

66

Thanks in large part to Prigogine's work during the past three decades, cross-cultural applications of chaos science have led to a new concept of time. As N. Katherine Hayles has written,

> Time is rarely represented any more as pointers across a mechanical clock's face; instead it is signified by the blinking display of an electronic clock. Similarly, time in fractal geometry is not treated as the advancement of points along a number line [or a number of lines of verse, as in the Elizabethan sonnet]. Rather it is conceptualized as small changes in the iterative formulae that are used to generate fractal shapes. . . . Changing these formulae only a little results in large-scale changes in the fractal forms. Consequently, complex shape changes can be described in many fewer bits of information than if one conceived of the shapes as masses of points that had to be advanced through time individually. Thus time still exists in fractal geometry . . . But it is no longer analogous to human movement through a Cartesian plane.[9]

For Hayles, in other words, fractal moments are examples of what Bohm calls allowable forms of discontinuous, or nonlinear time.[10]

Charles Olson calls to mind Ilya Prigogine's concept of a second time, an internal time, when he speaks of the need for poets to be aware of "motion inside of time" while avoiding in their verse Newtonian time-measures which can be tracked "by, (*sic*) the metronome."[11] In like manner, in an early volume of poetry entitled *After Lorca*, Jack Spicer insisted that "A poet is a time mechanic."[12] As an occasional member of the San Francisco Renaissance group of writers, many of whom were influenced by Olson's ideas, the Berkeley-based Spicer meant that for many writers of his generation, time was part of the creative apparatus of open form poetics.

The twentieth-century French poet Paul Valery has been quoted as saying, "Time is construction." What's especially noteworthy here is that it is the scientists

Ilya Prigogine and Isabelle Stengers who call on Valéry in their effort to describe nonlinear time in physics—a concept which, they insist, "carries a message that goes beyond science proper."[13]

What constitutes the praxes of nonlinear time in poetry? Here it's helpful, I think, to contrast the time mechanics of poems written in historical periods which themselves are characterized by differing cultural hermeneutics of time. First, a Shakespearian sonnet from the seventeenth century:

> Let me not to the marriage of true minds
> Admit impediments. Love is not love
> Which alters when it alteration finds,
> Or bends with the remover to remove.
> O no! it is an ever-fixed mark
> That looks on tempests and is never shaken;
> It is the star to every wand'ring bark,
> Whose worth's unknown, although his height be taken.
> Love's not Time's fool, though rosy lips and cheeks
> Within his bending sickle's compass come;
> Love alters not with his brief hours and weeks,
> But bears it out even to the edge of doom.
>> If this be error and upon me proved,
>> I never writ, nor no man ever loved.

Compare to the following poem from Jack Spicer's *Language*, first published as an individual volume in 1965:

> Love is not mocked whatever use
>> you put to it. Words are also not mocked.
> The soup of real turtles flows through
>> our veins. Being a /poet/ a
>> disyllable in a world of monosyllables.
>> Awakened by the distance between
>> the /o/ and the /e/

>The earth quakes. John F. Kennedy
>>is assassinated. The dark forest
>>of words lets in some light from
>>its branches. Mocking them,
>>the deep leaves
>That time leaves us
>Words, loves.[14]

At first glance both poems appear to be saying similar things: "Love is not love/Which alters when it alteration finds . . ." echoes "Love is not mocked whatever use you put to it." Love is represented in both poems as a constant. In fact, however, the time mechanics of both poems are shockingly different. Shakespeare's Sonnet 116 represents a linear progression, an argument, from one point to the next. Up to the final couplet, the rhyme scheme, abab, cdcd, efef, follows the breakdown of the triadic argument precisely.

The poem thus falls into four parts: the *exordium*, lines 1-4; the *narratio*, lines 5-8; the *confirmatio/refutatio*, lines 9-12; and the *peroratio*, lines 13-14. The first four lines, the *exordium*, tell us what love is not; the second, the *narratio*, tell us what love is; the *confirmatio/refutatio* tell us what love is not again; and then the couplet, which threatens the logic of the poem by a tautology—proving that love exists even beyond the logic of the poem itself. The last line says in essence: If love doesn't exist, then no man ever loved. The proof of the poem is maddeningly ironical, suggesting that love's logic is a slippery thing indeed. And yet in sending up the logic of classical discourse so well-loved by the Renaissance, Shakespeare, like John Donne after him, uses the logic himself.

Spicer's poem pursues love into a different universe. Like countless other post-Poundian verses, the lyric bounces from line to line unevenly. Rather than reading it from start to finish like Shakespeare's sonnet, we're obliged to make leaps from one line to the next in a nervous field of language, where even the words threaten to fly apart ("the distance between the [o] and the [e]"). One has the uneasy feeling that the poem is writing itself, that no one's in charge, that no predictable pattern in time can be established. On the contrary, Shakespeare's sonnet has built-in time signifiers clearly telling the reader where the poem will go: iambs in a line, rhymes at the ends of lines, stresses. "Love is not mocked" zigs and zags through its open field ending in syntactical ambiguity of the most radical sort: "Mocking them, the deep leaves/That time leaves us/Words, loves." For Spicer, in opposition to Shakespeare, "the future," as Prigogine and Isabelle Stengers say of nonlinear dynamics, "is not given."[15]

The time mechanics of Shakespeare's sonnet are classical in the sense that, as in classical physics, the poem moves the reader through what David Bohm calls "a continuous series of intermediate states in every transition."[16] That is to say, the poem's elegant rhetorical continuity shifts from *exordium*, to *narratio*, to *refutatio/confirmatio*, to *peroratio*. The first twelve lines fall into three sentences of four lines each, leading the reader through a continuous series of intermediate states to the couplet, where the demonstrative pronoun *this* makes of the first twelve lines a sort of gigantic antecedent, and provides the precise transition between the logic of the discourse and the tautological ending. The first point of contrast we may note between linear and nonlinear time mechanics, then, is that continuity in time is replaced by discontinuity.

A second point of contrast may be seen in the fractured grammar of the last three lines of "Love is not mocked": "Mocking them, the deep leaves/That time leaves us/Words, loves." The classical subject-verb-direct object-indirect object structure of linear time in "John throws the ball to Phil" gets lost in the maze of Spicer's syntactical ambiguity, where nonlinear time obliges the reader to immerse himself, willy-nilly, in the grammatical chaos of a fragment. The reader must ask himself, if "leaves" in the first line is the subject of the sentence, then where is the verb? "Leaves" in the second line is a verb, with time as its subject, so that "leaves" as a verb doesn't agree with "leaves" as a subject. Such a grammatical agreement would sound ludicrous, so the reader must look again. Might "loves," the last word of the poem, be the verb of the subject "leaves"? But "leaves" is a plural noun, and "loves"—if it can be taken as a verb—is singular. "Loves," of course, appears to be a noun anyway, like "words." The verb that conventionally keeps time in a classic English sentence, moving the words in linear progression, is missing.

Nor is there a happy marriage of linear time and logic in Spicer's poem as there is in Shakespeare's sonnet. The conclusion of "Love is not mocked" isn't a neat Elizabethan couplet but is composed of two words which express the bare essence of being. "Words, loves," makes no logical sense, sums up no argument, nor is meant to. Nowhere in Spicer's poem is there a linear one-to-one connection between sound and sense such as one finds in *The Two Noble Kinsmen* or, one might add, in the famous line from *Hamlet* spoken to Horatio by the dying prince, "And in this harsh world draw thy breath in pain/To tell my story," which mimics in its harsh spondaic measure the drum tattoo one might expect to hear at Hamlet's own funeral.

Nonlinear irreversible time is redundant in Shakespeare's sonnet because its time mechanics aren't *sui generis* —i.e., every Shakespeare sonnet keeps roughly the same time-measures and durations in line-length (14 lines), rhyme scheme (ab, ab, cd, cd, etc.), and syllables (10, 11, or 12 per line: iambs and variations). The time mechanics of Spicer's "Love is not mocked," however, are unique, discontinuous, an invention *of* the poem rather than a structure brought *to* the poem, as in Shakespeare's case. Line length varies in Spicer, as does syllabication, stress-patterns, sound. Time is reversible in Shakespeare's sonnet, insofar as the lines follow a predictable symmetry forwards and backwards, a parameter of syllable length, measure, rhyme, and line length; this pattern is identical from lines 14-1 as it is from lines 1-14. Read backward, Shakespeare's iambs turn into trochees and his trochees into iambs. The beats-per-line when reversed are also approximately the same; thus symmetry is preserved. Spicer's poem, needless to say, cannot be reversed in this manner; no such symmetrical pattern emerges when we backtrack from lines 10-1. Thus, for Spicer, the time mechanics of "Love is not mocked" are irreversible.

Finally, from the perspective of time mechanics, Spicer's view of rhyme is also significant. Spicer dismisses rhyme as a "stiffening in time," or a device which constrains the invention, or construction, as Paul Valery puts it, of time in language.[17] For Spicer, a rhyme is a temporal parameter or scaffolding that hinders the dynamic play of language. So what is gained through the poetics of nonlinearity in verse? What results when we free up language from the webs of Newtonian closure, from Newtonian linear time? What prevents the reign of utter chaos? How, for Jack Spicer, is "nonequilibrium," in Prigogine's and Stengers's phrase, "a source of order"?[18]

In fact, in "Love is not mocked," Spicer retains a number of conventional formal tropes, including irony (". . . whatever use you put to it"), intertextuality (the offhand allusions to Lewis Carroll), repetition ("Mocked . . . mocked . . . Mocking"), and the pun ("leaves . . . leaves"). These formal devices and structures act as healthy checks and balances on the randomness that Spicer's nonlinear time mechanics impose on language. Nevertheless, in the end "Love is not mocked" plays by very different rules than does Shakespeare's Sonnet 116. According to these rules, as Spicer always insisted, the poem

. . . does not have to fit together. Like the pieces of a totally unfinished jigsaw puzzle my grandmother left in the bedroom when she died in the living room. The pieces of the poetry or of this love.[19]

NOTES

1. Frank O'Conner, "Work in Progress," in *Dubliners: Text, Criticism, and Notes*, eds. Robert Scholes and A. Walton Litz (New York: Viking, 1969), p. 306.

2. Wylie Sypher, *Loss of the Self in Modern Literature and Art* (New York: Vintage Books, 1962), pp. 79-80.

3. David Bohm, *Wholeness and the Implicate Order* (London: Routledge and Kegan Paul, 1980), p. 38.

4. Charles Olson, *Selected Writings* (New York: New Directions, 1966), pp. 35-36.

5. Bohm, *Wholeness and the Implicate Order*, p. 211.

6. Ilya Prigogine, *From Being to Becoming* (New York: W.H. Freeman and Company, 1980), p. 211.

7. *Ibid.*, p. 213.

8. *Ibid.*, p. 210.

9. N. Katherine Hayles, *Chaos Bound: Orderly Disorder in Contemporary Literature and Science* (Ithaca: Cornell University Press, 1990), p. 290.

10. Physicists often object to the rather sloppy ways in which the term "nonlinearity" is employed by interdisciplinary scholars, some of whom occasionally forget that nonlinearity is also a *mathematical* concept. As Stephen H. Kellert has written,

> Nonlinear terms involve algebraic or other more complicated functions of . . . system variables. For example, in a system with two variables x and y, expressions such as x^2 or $\sin(x)$ or $5xy$ would be nonlinear terms. These terms may stem from the inclusion of such factors as frictional forces or limits to biological populations. The nonlinearity of the equations usually renders a closed-form solution impossible. . . . After modeling a physical system with a set of equations, [chaos researchers]   do not concentrate on finding a formula that will make possible the exact prediction of a future state from a present one.

Kellert neatly sums up his definition of nonlinearity:

> As a qualitative study, chaos theory investigates a system by asking about the general character of its long term behavior, rather than seeking to arrive at numerical predictions about its exact future state. (*In the Wake of Chaos: Unpredictable Order in Dynamical Systems* [Chicago: University of Chicago Press, 1993], pp. 3-4).

But Kellert's remarks also beg an important question: is nonlinearity *first and foremost* a mathematical concept? Or is mathematical nonlinearity *itself* part of a matrix of *non-magisterial*—i.e., separate but equal—epistemologies that can be grouped together under the rubric of Chaos?

In a recent article in the interdisciplinary journal *Configurations*, Peter Weingart and Sabine Maasen tackle this very issue:

> . . . [W]e are of the opinion that one has to acknowledge the fact that chaos is both an all-pervasive concept and heterogenous with respect to its semantics and pragmatics. It can be found in a number of discourses with a number of meanings and a number of uses. Therefore, instead of lamenting over nonserious and ill-defined applications, one should seek to understand the ways in which chaos manages to be both all-pervasive and heterogenous.

Weingart and Maasen then propose a methodology:

> In terms of research strategy this means, first, to demarcate the discursive landscape of chaos and the calendar of its spread throughout intra- and extrascientific discourses; second, to scrutinize the mechanisms of meaning production within individual discourses; and third, to map the intra- and extradiscursive links provided by chaos so as to answer the question whether it may be assigned the role of a cultural matrix.
> ("The Order of Meaning: The Career of Chaos as a Metaphor," *Configurations* 5 [Fall 1997], pp. 463-520).

In seeking to explore what Weingart and Maasen call an extradiscursive connection between chaos science and chaos poetics, I've chosen to focus here on the transdisciplinary nature of nonlinearity with regard to time.

11. Charles Olson, "Projective Verse," in *The Poetics of the New American Poetry*, eds. Donald Allen and Warren Tallman (New York: Grove Press, 1973), p. 148.

12. Jack Spicer, *The Collected Books of Jack Spicer*, ed. Robin Blaser (Los Angeles: Black Sparrow Press, 1975), p. 25.

13. Ilya Prigogine and Isabelle Stengers, *Order Out of Chaos* (New York: Bantam, 1984), p. 301.

14. Spicer, *The Collected Books of Jack Spicer*, p. 243.

15. Prigogine and Stengers, *Order Out of Chaos*, p. 301.

16. Bohm, *Wholeness and the Implicate Order*, p. 128.

17.   Spicer, *The Collected Books of Jack Spicer*, p. 177.

18.   Prigogine and Stengers, *Order Out of Chaos*, p. 287.

19.   Spicer, *The Collected Books of Jack Spicer*, p. 176.

Part II

Complementarity

Complementarity Across the Disciplines

omplementarity describes a system or systems of mutually interdependent and irreconcilable relations. As a scientific way of knowing, it denies strictly classical notions of contradiction, either/or, and binary (or digital) oppositions. It was the Danish physicist Niels Bohr who, during the so-called "golden age" of modern physics—i.e., the first third of the twentieth century—first posited complementarity as an indispensable model for understanding quantum phenomena:

> The two views of the nature of light [wave and particle] are rather to be considered as different attempts at an interpretation of experimental evidence in which the limitation of the classical concepts is expressed in complementary ways . . . In fact, here again we are not dealing with contradictory but with complementary pictures of the phenomena which only together offer a natural generalization of the classical mode of description.[1]

Dugald Murdoch separates Bohr's generic recipe into three key ingredients:

> Two or more concepts of propositions may be said to be complementary in Bohr's sense if and only if:
> a) they are different in meaning, or predicate different properties;
> b) together, or jointly, they constitute a complete description or representation of a thing;
> c) they are mutually exclusive or incompatible either in a logical sense or in an empirical sense.[2]

When, as a recipient of the Danish Order of the Elephant,[3] Bohr chose the Chinese ying and yang symbol for his coat of arms, he acknowledged that complementarity wasn't *invented* or even *discovered* by modern physicists. In fact, as a true transdisciplinary episteme, complementarity pops up regularly in the work of philosophers, scientists, and artists.[4]   As Arkady Plotnitsky has written, "Complementarity . . . allows for a very broad spectrum of parallel and interactive engagements of theoretical structures."[5]

Plotnitsky's use of the term *interactive* indicates that, as manifested in individual disciplines such as science, art, and literature, complementarity contributes like the separate instruments in an orchestra to an extremely complex metaprocess of cognition *which cannot be fully understood without taking these different modes of expression into account.*   Like an oboe, a French horn, and a violin, each discipline, while unique, acts in harmony with the others in contributing to an overarching interactive orchestral design. The resultant "symphony" constitutes an isomorphism, or basic structure of thought.

In Western philosophy, complementarity first appears as a full-blown episteme[6] in the form of Bacon's classic paradox:

> The old age of the world . . . is the attribute of our own times, not of that earlier age in which the ancients lived; and which the ancients lived; and which, though in respect of us it was the older, yet in the rest of the world it was the younger.[7]

Stephen Jay Gould then applies Bacon's paradox of complementarity to the history of natural science:

> [In Bacon] we get different answers from two equally proper and justifiable vantage points. Trilobites are both young (looking up from the origin of multicellular life) and old (looking back from 1992). Both perspectives, from both ends, are 'correct'—and they do contradict.[8]

Gould's reading of the Baconian paradox is correct—up to the very last, that is, when he falls into the very Aristotelian trap he has sought to avoid. As H.H. Pattee reminds us, the notion of contradiction is utterly redundant to that of complementarity:

> [T]his duality of descriptive modes and their incompatibility should not be thought of as a contradiction in any sense. In fact, there is none since the two modes of perception are formally disjoint [sic] and contradiction can only occur within a single formal system.[9]

In twentieth-century painting, the Dutch modernist M.C. Escher is best-known for his complementary poetics of space, wherein opposites are "annealed into a seamless alloy" of architectural and organic forms, as Leonard Shlain puts it. Of one of Escher's signature works, *Sky and Water I*, Shlain observes,

> Beginning with the polar opposites of black and white, his repetitive figures of fish, birds, frogs, and salamanders undergo a gradual metamorphosis in the center until they emerge transformed on the other side. With such mute, elegant graphics, Escher repudiated a linchpin of Western logic established by Aristotle. To paraphrase Aristotle's position, if A is a fish and B is a bird, and A's are not B's, then A cannot be B. Escher slides right through this either/or dichotomy . . . to fashion paintings for the viewer containing complex ideas that could be visualized without the use of equations.[10]

A century before Escher, the visionary poet William Blake found complementarity helpful in his attempts to chart the ontological topographies of innocence and experience. According to Alfred Kazin, in Blake's systems of thought experience

> is the 'contrary' of innocence, not its negative. Contraries are phases of the doubleness of all existence in the mind of man; they reflect the unalterable condition of the human struggle.[11]

In short, Blake's contraries are not to be seen as contradictions, but as complementarities.[12]

Complementarity also finds its way into contemporary literary theory:

> There is a tendency to assume [undecidability] refers to readers who, when forced to decide between two or more equally plausible and conflicting readings motivated by the same text, throw up their hands and decide that the choice can't be made. But undecidability in fact debunks this whole notion of reading as a decision-making process carried out on texts by readers. . . . The poststructuralist concept of undecidability, we might say, deconstructs the either/or type distinctions or oppositions that structuralists and formalists have made between reader and text.[13]

Because one-to-one influence isn't the issue here, there's little need to engage in futile chicken and egg arguments about which came first: complementarity as a scientific episteme or complementarity as a literary, artistic or philosophical episteme. Indeed, as Guy Rotella has shown in a study of complementarity in the poetry of Robert Frost, sometimes it's difficult to know which is the chicken and which is the egg:

> [I]n 1930 Frost was finding in the new physics of the preceding twenty years important parallels to his own long consideration of the essential role of metaphor in thinking, making and knowing.

Nevertheless, Rotella adds,

> None of this is to claim that Frost was in a particular or direct way influenced by what he came to know of the physics of the 'teens and twenties. He was writing poems that can be described by the terms of indeterminacy, correspondence, and complementarity *long before he became aware of these concepts in science.* (italics added)[14]

Here, too, an interdisciplinary reading of the work of a major American writer indicates that isomorphic connections between the disciplines are at least as telling as those that result from direct influences. Which brings me to the subject at hand: complementarity as a structural isomorphism in the short fiction of Ernest Hemingway.

———————

NOTES

1. Niels Bohr, *Atomic Theory and the Description of Nature* (Cambridge: Cambridge University Press, 1934), p. 56.

2. Dugald Murdoch, *Niels Bohr's Philosophy of Physics* (Cambridge: Cambridge University Press, 1987), p. 60.

3. Bohr's coat of arms includes the Latin motto *Contraria sunt complementa* (Opposites are complementary) (see Guy Rotella, "Comparing Conceptions: Frost and Eddington, Heisenberg, and Bohr," *American Literature* 59 [May 1987]: 181).

4. Latter-day physicists have begun to question the validity of Bohr's interpretation of quantum phenomena. Bohr insisted that, as John Gribbin puts it, "[Y]ou will never see the light acting as wave and particle at the same time." But in at least one recently documented case, Bohr was proven wrong:

    > In 1992, Japanese researchers, carrying out an experiment devised by an Indian team, did just that. They observed individual photons exhibiting wave-like properties and particle-like properties at the same time. Just what this means for our understanding of the quantum world is, as yet, far from clear. The one certain thing is that it is bad news for the Copenhagen Interpretation in its standard form.
    > (*Schrödinger's Kittens and the Search for Reality: Solving the Quantum Mysteries* [Boston: Little, Brown, and Company, 1995], p. 115)

    Bas C. van Fraassen and Jill Sigman go even further than Gribbin: "Today there seems little hope of reinstating complementarity as the key to interpretation of physics" (George Levine, ed., *Realism and Representation: Essays on the Problem of Realism in Relation to Science, Literature, and Culture* [Madison: University of Wisconsin Press, 1993], p. 92.) These observations return us to the question I raised earlier in this essay. If a scientific theory is flawed (it should be kept in mind, by the way, that complementarity is only one cornerstone of the Copenhagen Interpretation of quantum mechanics), does this mean that it's automatically rendered invalid as a *transdisciplinary* episteme?

    Actually, there are two issues involved here. On the one hand, as the case of Frank Norris makes abundantly clear, bad science can indeed be transmuted into good art. The other thing to keep in mind is that transdisciplinary isomorphisms cannot be considered as eternal Absolute Truths. Rather, they should be seen as cognitive structures that humans bring *to* the raw material of experience in order to better understand it. This is *not* to say that reality is in the eye (or mind) of the beholder, but that our *descriptions* of reality and Reality itself are two different things. As separate but interconnected entities, they constitute as it were an epistemological dance, wherein different partners "lead" at different times. Put another way, and as the examples of Bacon, Blake, and Escher make abundantly clear, complementarity comes and goes; where it will appear (or disappear) next, nobody knows.

5.   Arkady Plotnitsky, *In the Shadow of Hegel: Complementarity, History, and the Unconscious* (Gainesville, Fla.: University Press of Florida, 1993), p. 48.

6.   Bacon's own epistemological avatars range from the Latin Bible (Book II *Esdras*) to the poems of Giordano Bruno. (See Stephen Jay Gould, *Dinosaur in a Haystack: Reflections in Natural History* [New York: Crown Publishing, 1995], p. 78.)

7.   Gould, *Dinosaur in a Haystack,* p. 78.

8.   *Ibid.,* p. 79.

9.   H.H. Pattee, "The Complementarity Principle in Biological and Social Structures," *Journal of Social and Biological Structures* I (April 1978): 193.

10.   Leonard Shlain, *Art and Physics: Parallel Visions in Space, Time, and Light* (New York: William Morrow, 1991), p. 242.

11.   Alfred Kazin, ed., *The Portable Blake* (New York: Viking, 1946), pp. 41-42.

12.   Because Blake distrusted and even despised science as a way of knowing the world, doubtless he would have been appalled to learn that complementarity would one day become a scientific episteme via the Copenhagen Interpretation of quantum mechanics. As Ifor Evans has written,

> Until the Eternal Man is awakened in Spiritual Freedom,
> Science and Analysis and Reason, that is Bacon, Locke, and
> Newton, are the enemies of vision. This view Blake
> expressed consistently for it is basic in his whole thought.
> (*Literature and Science* [London: George Allen & Unwin,
> Ltd., 1954], p. 35.)

13.   Ross C. Murfin, "What is Deconstruction?," in James Joyce, *The Dead: Case Studies in Contemporary Criticism*, ed. Daniel R. Schwartz (Boston: St. Martin's Press, 1994), p. 211.

14.   Rotella, "Comparing Conceptions: Frost and Eddington, Heisenberg, and Bohr," p. 184.

Ernest Hemingway and the Included Middle

I n the past, virtually all structural analyses of Hemingway's short stories have begun and ended with discussions of binary oppositions. Consider Joseph DeFalco's reading of the either/or dichotomies in "Hills Like White Elephants":

> The details of sun and shade, of heat and relief from heat, of barrenness and vegetation contrast the train station where the action takes place with the hills in the distance across the river.[1]

Following the lead of J.A. Greimas, David Lodge observes of Hemingway's "Cat in the Rain,"

> All concepts are semantically defined by a binary relationship with their opposites (e.g. Life/Death) or negatives (e.g. Life/Non-Life) yielding the basic semiotic model A : B : : -A-B (e.g. Life : Death : : Non-Life: Non-Death . . .)[2]

To be sure, Greimas's/Lodge's semiotic system for "Cat in the Rain" isn't as simple as DeFalco's conventional structural model for "Hills Like White Elephants," but their bias, like DeFalco's, is essentially a binary one. Even critical disagreements over the relationships between theme and structure in stories like "Cat in the Rain" tend to fall along binary lines. As Oddvar Holmesland has noted, "One critic [John V. Hagopian] regards the rain as a positive force, the other [David Lodge] takes it to be negative."[3]

Hemingway's lesser-known short fictions have also inspired a host of binary approaches. In an extended discussion of the neglected "Homage to Switzerland,"

Erik Nakjavani coins the phrase "essential transversal repetitions," or a system of oppositions which

> appear to derive as a series from a set of primary, inside versus outside binary oppositions (so common in Hemingway's fiction): warm versus cold, light versus darkness, movement versus stasis, manmade world versus natural world, order versus disorder, predictable versus unpredictable, known versus unknown, female versus male, heterosexual versus homosexual . . .[4]

In what follows I'll argue that, while they are of limited use as epistemological models which characterize the world of Hemingway's short fictions, such systems of binary oppositions—especially light versus dark, female versus male, and hetero- versus homosexual—are ultimately insufficient to render adequately the full, or *complementary*, richness of Hemingway's overall artistic vision.

A helpful way to grasp the dynamics of lexical complementarity is to contrast them with the classical (Aristotelian) and neo-classical (Cartesian) doctrines of *the excluded middle*. According to this familiar system of hermeneutics—of which the Cartesian split between mind and body is the best-known modern example—the world is constituted of either/or dualities. No middle ground, or excluded middle, can exist between them. Complementarity, like Aristotelian logic, also posits what James Gleick calls "an inescapable duality at the heart of things," but this duality is one of and/both, not of either/or.[5] Put another way, complementarity brings a radically new system of logic to the literary text—that of the *included* middle. Brian McHale elaborates:

> 'Excluded middles,' muses [Thomas Pynchon's] heroine Oedipa Maas, are 'bad shit, to be avoided.' She is lamenting the absence, in her world—as indeed in our world, according to conventional logics—of any *third alternative* to the polarity of true and false, any mode of being between existence and non-existence. (italics added)[6]

The third alternative McHale refers to is the logic of the included middle, or complementarity. Before proceeding any further, let me re-emphasize what complementarity *doesn't* mean. It doesn't mean that two "competing" propositions (mathematical, political, philosophical, psychological, or "literary") may be equally true (or false) at the same time. It means, rather, that two (or more) propositions that contradict each other *according to the either/or principle of Aristotelian logic* may be conjoined in what amounts to a new, not *il*logical but *a*logical way of knowing.

Some of Hemingway's ablest critics have already discovered a poetics of complementarity in the novels, where it plays a significant role in the too-often misunderstood politics of gender. As Rena Sanderson has written of *For Whom the Bell Tolls,*

> Maria is the female principle that complements Jordan's male nature; her qualities unite with his, and the idyllic love affair blossoms. Maria imagines that she and Jordan will be 'as one animal of the forest and be so close that neither one can tell that one of us is one and not the other.' In describing their lovemaking Hemingway invokes the cosmos. His incantatory verbal rendering of the sex act . . . suggests a transcendent fusion of the couple with each other and with the universe: 'for now always one now; one only one, there is no other one but now, one . . . one and one is one . . .'[7]

Bickford Sylvester has also noticed a pattern of complementarity in *Across the River and Into the Trees,* citing as one example Colonel Cantwell's description of Renata as "boy, daughter, or whatever it is."[8] So far as I know, however, Thomas Strychacz is the first scholar to take note of the presence of complementarity in Hemingway's shorter works, and then only in passing:

> In late 1924 and early 1925 . . . Hemingway began to envisage a new role for the vignettes [of *In Our Time*]. Interspersed between the short stories, the vignettes allowed Hemingway to exploit a typically

> modernist esthetics of fragmentation and juxtaposition. The rapid-fire exchange of story and inter-chapter in the new *In Our Time*, sometimes working by *complementary meanings* and sometimes by ironic counterpoint, drew on the collage technique of Pablo Picasso and George Braque [and] the film montage of Sergei Eisenstein . . . (italics added)[9]

Particularly noteworthy here is Strychacz's suggestion that "ironic counterpoint"—i.e., binary oppositions used for ironic purposes—begins to share the spotlight with the logic of the included middle as a key structural element in Hemingway's short narratives. In fact, lexical complementarity *includes, but also transcends*, contrapuntal structures. In many of the best-known stories from the twenties and thirties, complementarity gave the young writer a powerful tool to explore human relationships in search of rich new ironies and insights that the strict oppositional logic of excluded middles would have denied him.

Let me offer a working model for the thematic and structural dynamics of complementarity in what is perhaps Hemingway's most scrutinized short work, "A Clean, Well-Lighted Place." "Well-Lighted Place," of course, has long occupied a privileged place in the pantheon of Hemingway's so-called studies in fear (the phrase is F. Scott Fitzgerald's). Fear, or more precisely the psychology of fear, is manifested in the story in a number of different ways. These manifestations occupy two broad complementary categories, or what I'll call *presences* and *absences*. Simply put, the *presence* of fear cannot be understood or appreciated without taking into account the *absence* of fear and the way(s) in which it also creates meaning in the lives of characters in the story.

"A Clean, Well-Lighted Place" is not simply "about" the psychology of fear. Rather, the different forms of fear are used by Hemingway as *architectural building blocks*, making of theme and structure a seamless whole, and making of "Well-Lighted Place" a profoundly organic work of art. As a *structural* entity, the complementary architectonics of fear subsume all binary oppositions (*e.g.*, light *vs.* dark, man-made *vs.* natural), beckoning us to enter instead an ontological limbo of the self, a complex world not of either/or but of both/and.

The architectonics of fear in "A Clean, Well-Lighted Place" may be diagrammed as follows:

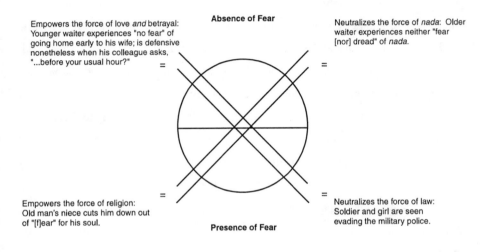

Absence of Fear

Empowers the force of love *and* betrayal: Younger waiter experiences "no fear" of going home early to his wife; is defensive nonetheless when his colleague asks, "...before your usual hour?"

Neutralizes the force of *nada*: Older waiter experiences neither "fear [nor] dread" of *nada*.

Empowers the force of religion: Old man's niece cuts him down out of "[f]ear" for his soul.

Neutralizes the force of law: Soldier and girl are seen evading the military police.

Presence of Fear

Figure 1

At the heart of this intricate system of complementary presences and absences is the nada prayer of the philosophical and kindly older waiter:

> Our nada who art in nada, nada be thy name thy kingdom nada thy will be nada in nada as it is in nada. Give us this nada our daily nada and nada us our nada as we nada our nadas and nada us not into nada but deliver us from nada; pues nada. Hail nothing full of nothing, nothing is with thee.[10]

Scholarly assessments of the philosophical implications of the prayer often gloss over, or completely ignore, its equally important preamble:

> It was a nothing that he knew too well. It was all a nothing and a man was nothing too. It was only that and light was all it needed and a certain cleanness and order.[11]

A complementary reading of the curiously-worded line "light was all it needed" helps to reveal the hidden complexities of the nada prayer that follows. One interpretation is that light is *necessary* to keep nada at bay. Another is that light is *sufficient* to keep nada at bay. A third interpretation, however, problematizes both of these: *nada needs light.* Light is necessary, not simply to keep nada at bay, but to convert it into the milk of human kindness, even as light in the natural world energizes the production of food through photosynthesis. According to this tertiary reading of the line "light was all it needed," nada is a source of compassion and charity on the part of the older waiter himself, for it's the presence of the absence of *nada* that moves him "to keep the cafe open for all those who need a light for the night."[12] Such a reading also helps us to understand why Hemingway balances the oppositional compound sentence, "The light is very good and also, now, there are shadows of the leaves," with the complementary *and* instead of the binary *but*.[13]

Critical debates concerning the meaning of *nada* are commonly divided into two camps. According to one, nada is negative, an emblem of despair that is concretized by the chaotic darkness surrounding the well-lit, orderly Spanish cafe. According to the other, nada challenges the older waiter to reflect on what it means to be human; thus his duties at the cafe comprise so many existential errands, symptomatic of what Jean-Paul Sartre termed the far side of despair. From this reverse critical angle, "A Clean, Well-Lighted Place" sounds a note of affirmation, albeit in a minor key. As Richard B. Hovey puts it,

> There is no God, no Father, no mother to watch over us. But despite the all-surrounding night of nada—*in fact because of it*—the older waiter sees the need to share with others whatever there is of kindly light. (italics added)[14]

Hovey is correct to suggest that *nada* redeems a charitable impulse on the part of the older waiter who is willing to stay open "because there may be some one who needs the cafe."[15] On the other hand, there's much more to the complex psychology of "A Clean, Well-Lighted Place" than a Manichean struggle between the signifiers light (the older waiter's kindness) and dark (the "nothing full of nothing" that is always "with thee").[16] In fact, a story justly renowned for its "unsuspected depths"[17] cannot be strictly categorized as (1) embodying a "totally affirmative"[18] theme or as (2) positing "a perfect, but negative, vacuum."[19] Philosophical analogs like Blavatsky's "He who would hear the voice of Nada . . . and comprehend it . . . hast become the light"[20] do call a Manichean hermeneutics into question, but such nineteenth-century mysticism seems ultimately foreign to Hemingway's modernist temperament.

In the opening scene of "A Clean, Well-Lighted Place," the old man "sits in the shadow the leaves of the tree made against the electric light."[21] This positioning indicates that to interpret the man-made light solely as a positive force, and the natural darkness of nada as a negative one, is insufficient. As Hovey points out, the older waiter is moved to keep the light on not simply in spite of nada but also because of it; it's this presence of absence that creates the story's "ironic paradox," in Jackson J. Benson's phrase, wherein "only through the awareness of nothing or non-meaning can meaning be created."[22]

But man-made light is also an enemy to man. It's the street light that "shines on the brass number" of the passing soldier's collar, illuminating him and making him and the girl he's with vulnerable to arrest.[23] Thus, the light and shadow of "A

92

Clean, Well-Lighted Place" *both* partake of negative and positive values. In effect, the story mirrors itself in what H.H. Pattee calls "a paradoxical articulation of two modes of knowing."[24]

This complementary, or dyadic, principle of mirroring is articulated in the infrastructure of "A Clean, Well-Lighted Place" as a series of double chiasmuses. A: The old man asks the younger waiter for "another brandy," while the barman in the bodega asks the older waiter if he wishes "another copita." B: The younger waiter refuses the old man's request, while the older waiter refuses the barman's offer. Or, A: The old man counts the saucers "slowly," while the older waiter is slow to leave the cafe. B: The soldier and the girl "hurried" past the cafe, while the younger waiter is "in a hurry" to leave the cafe.[25] These self-erasing chiasmuses also function as lexical supports in the architectonics of nada.

The fictional realm of "A Clean, Well-Lighted Place" is divided into four kingdoms of force: the force of law, the force of religion, the force of love and/or betrayal, and the force of nada. These forces correspond precisely to Hemingway's use of time to advance the plot at four critical junctures in the story: the allusion to the old man's suicide attempt (the past: *religion*), the passing of the soldier and the girl (the present: *law*), the younger waiter's plans for the rest of the night (the future: *love and/or betrayal*), and the older waiter's meditation on nada that transcends human space and human time. (See Figure 1.)

Like the needle of a compass, the older waiter's ambiguous smile ("Hail nothing, full of nothing, nothing is with thee. He smiled. . .") points to all four kingdoms of force.[26] It echoes the "joke" the older waiter makes when he suggests to the younger waiter that going home to his wife "before your usual hour" might not be such a good idea.[27] It also appears to signify mockery or even blasphemy, coming as it does immediately after the *nada* prayer. In addition, the smile serves to *amplify the ambiguities* established earlier in the story when, as the soldier and the girl hurry past in the incriminating light, one pessimistic waiter says, "The guard will pick him up," while the other optimistic waiter responds, "What does it matter if he gets what he's after?"[28] Since Hemingway seems to have deliberately made it impossible to assign dialogue at this point in the story,[29] the older waiter's smile later on may be also interpreted in complementary fashion—namely as *pessimistic and optimistic at the same time.* Finally, the smile may also signify stoic wisdom—even benign acceptance—on the part of the compassionate older waiter.

In the hands of an artist like Hemingway, a poetics of complementarity is not limited to matters of setting, structure, plot, dialogue, and syntax; it may also embrace the melopoeaic meaning(s) of a single word—what Robert Frost called the sound of sense. Of the last line of Frost's "Stopping By Woods on a Snowy Evening" ("And miles to go before I sleep"), Guy Rotella asks, "[i]s the repeated word a rhyme? Is the resolution excessive; does the repeated line work as a sign of *forced* closure? None of this is resolved; it is kept in complementary suspension."[30] As for the poem's equally familiar first line ("Whose woods these are I think I know"), Rotella adds,

> As an expression of doubtful guessing, 'think' opposes 'know,' with its air of certitude. The line might be read to emphasize doubt (Whose woods these are I *think* I know) or confident knowledge (Whose woods these are I think I *know*). Once the issue is introduced, even a scrupulously 'neutral' reading points it up.[31]

If we choose to stress Frost's own use of the modal verb *must* in the fifth line ("My little horse must think it queer"), as in *has to*, nature on a snowy night becomes blindly deterministic, different from and indifferent to the human sensibilities of the speaker. If we distill the sound in a different way, however, the opposite happens; an unstressed *must* suggests that nature accepts the narrator as a thinking being, a part

94

of the cosmic whole. It's this *second*, equally legitimate *must* of "Stopping By Woods" that, as Rotella writes, "gives the game [of complementarity] away."[32]

I wish to make the same claim for Hemingway's use of the modal verb *must* in "A Clean, Well-Lighted Place" as does Rotella in his discussion of complementarity in Robert Frost's best-known poem. For the prosodic status of the last line of "Well-Lighted Place"— "Many must have it"—is strikingly similar to that of the fifth line of "Stopping by Woods."[33] One may emphasize the subject and *de-emphasize* the modal verb, as in *Many* must have it, where *it* signifies a bleak existential condition shared by others. According to this reading, the reappearance of the indefinite *it* connects insomnia with the darksome nada of the older waiter's revised Lord's Prayer. But there's no reason *not* to emphasize the modal, as in Many *must* have it, where *it* now signifies manna for being. In *both* cases, nada —to paraphrase Martin Heidegger—appears a necessary way to be for humans. Like the owner of Robert Frost's snowy woods, it has no face, but wears many complementary masks, one of which is a Spanish waiter's tired smile.

If we ask, therefore, What is the truth behind the older waiter's smile, the answer is, *there isn't any*; if we ask, What is the bottom line (or bottom lines) to "A Clean, Well-Lighted Place," the answer is, *there isn't any*. Once again, we need to keep in mind what a complementary reading *doesn't* entail. Of course, works of fiction can and do accommodate alternate readings, even when these readings flatly contradict each other. But this pluralistic (or relativistic) principle isn't necessarily synonymous with the principle of complementarity. Complementarity dictates, rather, that the story constitutes not the sum of its meanings (even when the story may be said to be larger than the sum of its parts) but the remainder of its meanings. *The remainder is always zero.* In Wallace Stevens's idiom, this fecund zero is *the nothing that is* as opposed to *the nothing that is not*.[34] Put another way, complementarity presupposes not the absence of meaning but the presence of non-meaning. To comprehend this crucial distinction with regard to "A Clean, Well-Lighted Place" is to comprehend the suave and supple metaphysics of nada.

Complementarity also enables us to read a number of Hemingway's stories as chapters in a metanarrative bound together by the alogic of both/and, as opposed to the logic of either/or. The complementarity group includes "The Killers," "Hills Like White Elephants," "Soldier's Home," "The Sea Change," "A Canary for One," and, of course, "A Clean, Well-Lighted Place." In thematic terms, each of these works features an included middle consisting of states of *becoming* rather than *being*.

Complementarity does much more than govern the world of these short fictions like an overarching cosmic principle. Ontological states of in-betweenness also come about as the result of a given character's false perception that reality consists solely of binary oppositions. Thus, Harold Krebs in "Soldier's Home" is caught in a trap between desire and memory, between the Scylla of wanderlust and the Charybdis of nostalgia, because he thinks only in terms of the "truths" of the past and the "lies" of the present.[35] Nick Adams in "The Killers" naively assumes that he will substitute some future happiness for the past horrors of Summit when he tells George hopefully, "I'm going to get out of this town" ("That's a good thing to do," George replies ironically).[36] And the man in "Hills Like White Elephants" mistakenly imagines that "We'll be fine afterward" (after his lover Jig agrees to have an abortion).[37]

Not surprisingly, most of the major characters in the complementarity group are frozen in the middle of a journey. Nick Adams will keep moving from one town to another; the deracinated Krebs will "go to Kansas City";[38] Jig and her American lover will continue their trip to Madrid. In like manner, most of the action in "A Canary for One" takes place on a Paris-bound *rapide*, while the unnamed girl in "The

Sea Change" (who is between lovers) and the older waiter in "A Clean, Well-Lighted Place" are last seen leaving a bar and a bodega, respectively.

From the vantages of narrative poetics (the use of unreliable narrators like Jake Barnes in *The Sun Also Rises* and Frederic Henry in *A Farewell to Arms*); of plot development (the famous principle of the iceberg in classic short works like "Big, Two-Hearted River"); of setting (the bars and cafes of Paris and Pamplona in *The Sun Also Rises*); and of tone (the ironically "objective" attitudes toward the horrors of war in the interchapters of *In Our Time*), Hemingway's niche in the annals of Modernism has long been secure. A poetics of complementarity reveals still another side to the Modernist bias of Hemingway's early work.

Before the turn of the twentieth century, Matthew Arnold had written in one of his best-known poems,

> Wandering between two worlds, one dead,
> The other powerless to be born,
> With nowhere yet to rest my head,
> . . . on earth I wait forlorn.[39]

For Arnold, "nowhere" consisted of an included middle—a twilight zone of the spirit in which his latter-day Victorian imagination was obliged to roam fortuitously like a soul in search of a body. A generation later, T.S. Eliot sounded the same somber note of complementarity in "The Hollow Men":

> Between the idea
> And the reality
> Between the motion
> And the act
> Falls the Shadow . . .

> Between the conception
> And the creation
> Between the emotion
> And the response
> Falls the Shadow. . . [40]

Some of Eliot's best-known *dramatis personae*, notably Tiresias from *The Waste Land*, wander these ontological shadowlands of the in-between. The essence of Tiresias's being *is* complementarity:

> . . . when the human engine waits
> Like a taxi throbbing waiting,
> I Tiresias, though blind, *throbbing between two lives*,
> Old man with wrinkled female breasts, can see . . .
> (italics added)[41]

Like Eliot's Tiresias, Phil, the co-protagonist of Hemingway's "The Sea Change," suffers the agonies of the damned because virtually every person in the story is "a potential metamorph of himself."[42] In describing Phil's acute ontological dilemma, Warren Bennett all but employs the term "complementarity":

> Having accepted as correct [his lover's] 'logic' that 'Vice and virtue there is none at all' and that a sexual act is a sexual act—distinctions in gender are invalid—Phil has changed from 'brown young man' [sic] to a 'girl,' no different from the woman to whom the girl is now going, and, by the same logic, no different from the male prostitutes—the girls—standing beside him at the bar. The unresolvable contradiction for Phil, and the reason why he says that vice is a 'very strange thing,' is that his sexual indulgences with the girl and his acceptance of the girl's logic have made him, in effect, one with the waiting lesbian and one with the homosexuals, when, in fact, he is not one with them and can never be one with them.[43]

Matthew Arnold would have been shocked by the subject matter of stories like "The Sea Change," but he would have also understood the ontological basis for Phil's crisis of self. The creator of *The Waste Land*'s infinitely suffering Tiresias understood it too. Clearly, Hemingway wasn't alone among writers and poets of the modern era in intuiting complementarity as a painful way of knowing and experiencing the world.

Hemingway's Modernist credentials notwithstanding, some critics have pinpointed intriguing *post*modern moments in both the long and short works. "Postmodernists are beginning to recognize," Michael Reynolds points out, "that Hemingway's texts, above or below the waterline, are frequently concerned with the [postmodernist] problems of the writer writing."[44] Specifically, Lawrence Broer sees reflected in the posthumously published novel *The Garden of Eden* "Hemingway's interest in the postmodern theme of subjective reality—reality as artifice . . . ."[45] From the short canon, "The Natural History of the Dead" has been interpreted by Charles Stetter and Gerald Locklin as an early example of metafiction.[46]

As we've seen, Thomas Pynchon's Oedipa Maas in *The Crying of Lot 49* thinks of a logic of excluded middles as "bad shit, to be avoided." Interestingly, we might expect many characters from the complementarity group of short fictions—Nick Adams and Harold Krebs, say—to make the same observation about *in*cluded middles, since complementarity is so clearly for them a dreadful state. What matters isn't so much that complementarity can mean very different things for a Modernist author like Hemingway and a Postmodernist author like Pynchon, but that complementarity strengthens the case for former as an important transitional figure in twentieth-century American fiction.

But why should *Hemingway* —as opposed to other literary contemporaries like (say) F. Scott Fitzgerald—find this particular mode of interpreting the complexities of human experience so appealing? On the other hand, if we recall another key ingredient in Jackson J. Benson's esthetic recipe for Hemingway's short fiction—the dark channels of Hemingway's personality—the real question is, why *shouldn't* Hemingway have been attracted to complementarity as a way of understanding human nature?[47] As recent biographical criticism has convincingly demonstrated, in the very fiber of his emotional being Hemingway embodied the essence of complementarity by resisting the fundamental binary (and biological) logic that a human being cannot be a man and a woman at the same time.

Thanks to the pioneering work of scholars like Robert Scholes and Nancy R. Comley, and especially that of the biographers Kenneth S. Lynn and Mark Spilka, it's been established beyond doubt that Ernest Miller Hemingway

> was raised androgynously by parents peculiarly steeped in the conflicting codes of manhood that were vying for sway in the late nineteenth century and that would continue to press their rival claims upon him throughout his lifetime.[48]

Even the very young Ernest intuited that a terrible emotional conflict was befalling him, one that would last to the end of his life and almost certainly play a part in his suicide in Idaho in 1961. If he was obliged to dress up like his older sibling Marcelline, and thus play "the part of his sister's sister," as Kenneth S. Lynn puts it, Hemingway the little boy also resisted, gamely and poignantly, the attempt to transubstantiate his gender:

> Even minor frustrations of his will to be a boy could cause him to slap his mother, and one day he symbolically shot her. She called him her Dutch dolly, as was her wont, but this time the feminine epithet triggered an outburst of sexual rage. 'I not a Dutch dolly. I Pawnee Bill. Bang, I shoot Fweetee [Hemingway's childhood nickname for his mother Grace].' He also was much given to shooting Marcelline, who was supposed to 'fall down dead' every time.[49]

During the vulnerable years of his boyhood, in other words, complementarity was for Ernest Hemingway *a way to be*. It was inevitable that this ontological "wound of androgyny," in Spilka's phraseology, should eventually find its way into his adult life—and into his writing.[50]

NOTES

1.   Joseph DeFalco, *The Hero in Hemingway's Short Stories* (Pittsburgh: University of Pittsburgh Press, 1963), p. 170.

2.   David Lodge, "Analysis and Interpretation of the Realist Text: A Pluralistic Approach to Hemingway's 'A Cat in the Rain,' " *Poetics Today* 4 (Summer 1980): 6.

3.   Oddvar Holmesland, "Structuralism and Interpretation: Ernest Hemingway's 'A Cat in the Rain,' " in *New Critical Approaches to the Short Stories of Ernest Hemingway,* ed. Jackson J. Benson (Durham: Duke University Press, 1990), p. 64.

4.   Erik Nakjavani, "Repetition as Design and Intention: Hemingway's 'Homage to Switzerland,' " in *Hemingway's Neglected Short Fiction: New Perspectives*, ed. Susan F. Beegel (Tuscaloosa: University of Alabama Press, 1989), p. 266.

5.   James Gleick, *Genius* (New York: Vintage, 1992), p. 106.

6.   Brian McHale, *Postmodernist Fiction* (New York: Methuen, 1987), p. 106.

7.   Rena Sanderson, "Hemingway and Gender History," in *The Cambridge Companion to Hemingway*, ed. Scott Donaldson (New York: Cambridge University Press, 1996), pp.188-89.

8.   Bickford Sylvester, "The Cuban Context of *The Old Man and the Sea*," in *The Cambridge Companion to Hemingway*, p. 266.

9.   Thomas Strychacz, *"In Our Time*, Out of Season," in *The Cambridge Companion to Hemingway*, p. 60.

10.   Ernest Hemingway, *The Short Stories of Ernest Hemingway* (New York: Scribners, 1938), p. 383.

11.   *Ibid.*, p. 383.

12.   *Ibid.*, p. 382.

13.   *Ibid.*, p. 382.

14.   Richard B. Hovey, *Hemingway: The Inward Terrain* (Seattle: University of Washington Press, 1968), p. 25.

15.   Hemingway, *The Short Stories of Ernest Hemingway*, p. 382.

16.   *Ibid.*, pp. 382, 383.

17.   Sean O'Faolain, " 'A Clean, Well-Lighted Place,' " in *Hemingway: A Collection of Critical Essays*," ed. Robert P. Weeks (Englewood Cliffs, N.J.: Prentice Hall, Inc., 1962), p. 112.

18. Annette Benert, "Survival Through Irony: Hemingway's 'A Clean, Well-Lighted Place.' " *Studies in Short Fiction* 11 (1974): 187.

19. Sam Bluefarb, "The Search for the Absolute in Hemingway's 'A Clean, Well-Lighted Place' and 'The Snows of Kilamanjaro,' " *Bulletin of the Rocky Mountain MLA* 25 (1971): 5.

20. Ely Stock, "Nada in Hemingway's 'A Clean, Well-Lighted Place,' " *Midcontinent American Study Journal* 3 (Spring 1962): 54.

21. Hemingway, *The Short Stories of Ernest Hemingway*, p. 379.

22. Jackson J. Benson, ed., *New Critical Approaches to the Short Stories of Ernest Hemingway* (Durham: Duke University Press, 1990), p. 117.

23. Hemingway, *The Short Stories of Ernest Hemingway*, p. 379.

24. H.H. Pattee, "The Complementarity Principle in Biological and Social Structures," *Journal of Social and Biological Structures* I (April 1978): 192.

25. Hemingway, *The Short Stories of Ernest Hemingway*, pp. 381, 383, 381, 379, 382.

26. *Ibid.*, p. 383.

27. *Ibid.*, p. 383.

28. *Ibid.*, p. 379.

29. In a laudable attempt to clear up an ongoing debate concerning which of the two waiters is speaking in the early going of "A Clean, Well-Lighted Place," Joseph F. Gabriel argued a generation ago that "the story does not support any consistent interpretation ("The Logic of Confusion in Hemingway's 'A Clean, Well-Lighted Place,' " *College English* 22 [May 1961]: 540.) A legitimate case can be made, in other words, for *both* waiters speaking the lines of dialogue assigned to each one. Moreover, Gabriel adds, this ambiguity is not the result of carelessness or happenstance:

> [W]e have here one of the most artfully contrived pieces in the Hemingway canon . . . the inconsistency of the dialogue is deliberate, an integral part of the meaning actualized in the story (540).

In Gabriel's view, the interchangeability of dialogue and speaker(s) is a brilliant ploy by Hemingway to prepare readers for a close encounter with nada, an entity that encompasses the world views of *both* waiters. Although the waiters are of "two different kinds," their differences are complementary rather than binary (Hemingway, *The Short Stories of Ernest Hemingway*, p. 382).

If Gabriel is right (as I think he is) in arguing that the ambiguity of who says what early on exists by design, then the line, ". . . he [the older waiter] continued the conversation with himself" is significant (382). From this vantage, the waiters are counterparts, younger and older editions of the same person. After "putting up the shutters" together, they echo each other's "good night," whereupon the older waiter continues "the conversation" as though his colleague were still there—which, ontologically speaking, he is (382).

In any case, I can't accept all of a pieceWarren Bennett's contention that the structure of "A Clean, Well-Lighted Place" is "based on a consistent polarity: 'despair,' characterized by depth of feeling and insight into the human condition, in opposition to 'confidence,' characterized by a lack of feeling and, therefore, a lack of insight" ("Character, Irony, and Resolution: 'A Clean, Well-Lighted Place,' " in *The Short Stories of Ernest Hemingway: Critical Essays*, ed. Jackson J. Benson [Durham: Duke University Press, 1975], p. 262.). And while I agree with Gabriel's pronouncement that the ambiguous nature of nada buttresses an interpretation of purposeful ambiguity in the waiters' opening dialogue, Gabriel unfortunately abandons complementarity at the precise point where the story most demands it: "The light stands in direct contrast to the attributes which so overwhelmingly prevail in the universe outside" (541). My central argument is that this reading is inadequate to interpret the story *as a whole*.

30.	Guy Rotella, "Comparing Conceptions: Frost and Eddington, Heisenberg, and Bohr," *American Literature* 59 (May 1987): 187.

31.	*Ibid.*, p. 187.

32.	*Ibid.*, p. 187.

33.	Hemingway, *The Short Stories of Ernest Hemingway*, p. 383.

34.	See Stevens's poem "The Snow Man," in Wallace Stevens, *The Palm at the End of the Mind: Selected Poems and a Play*, ed. Holly Stevens (New York: Vintage, 1972), p. 54.

35.	Hemingway, *The Short Stories of Ernest Hemingway*, p. 4.

36.	*Ibid.*, p. 289.

37.	*Ibid.*, p. 275.

38.	*Ibid.*, p. 153.

39.	Matthew Arnold, "Stanzas from the Grand Chartreuse," *The Major Victorian Poets: Tennyson, Browning, Arnold*, ed. William E. Buckler (New York: Houghton Mifflin, 1973), pp. 608-09.

40.	T.S. Eliot, *Collected Poems 1909-1962* (New York: Harcourt, Brace and World, 1963), pp. 81-82.

41.	*Ibid.*, pp. 61-62.

42.	Daniel Albright, *Quantum Poetics: Yeats, Pound, Eliot, and the Science of Modernism* (New York: Cambridge University Press, 1997), p. 238.

43.	Warren Bennett, " 'That's Not Very Polite': Sexual Identity in Hemingway's 'The Sea Change,' " in *Hemingway's Neglected Short Fiction: New Perspectives*, p. 238.

44.   Michael Reynolds, "*A Farewell to Arms*: Doctors in the House of Love," in *The Cambridge Companion to Hemingway*, p. 112.

45.   Lawrence Broer, "Hemingway's 'On Writing': A Portrait of the Artist as Nick Adams," *Hemingway's Neglected Short Fiction: New Perspectives*, p. 133.

46.   Charles Stetler and Gerald Locklin, " 'A Natural History of the Dead' as Metafiction," in *Hemingway's Neglected Short Fiction: New Perspectives*, p. 249.

47.   Jackson J. Benson, ed., *New Critical Approaches to the Short Stories of Ernest Hemingway* (Durham: Duke University Press, 1990), p. 288.

48.   Mark Spilka, *Hemingway's Quarrel with Androgyny* (Lincoln: University of Nebraska Press, 1990), p. 330.

49.   Kenneth S. Lynn, *Hemingway* (New York: Simon and Schuster, 1987), p. 44.

50.   *Ibid.*, p. 13.

"It was no accident," Lynn adds,

> that from 'Soldier's Home' to 'The Last Good Country'
> [Hemingway] would write about tomboyish girls, or that he
> was sexually attracted to Jinny Pfeiffer and Gertrude Stein, or
> that he valued Hadley—as he would his other wives—as a
> good buddy who could drink with him and share his sporting
> enthusiasms. (322)

Hemingway's Canary for None: "A Canary for One"

Structural approaches to "A Canary for One" usually focus on binary oppositions which include, but aren't limited to, physical settings and patterns of chiaroscuro. As Scott Donaldson points out, these contrasts are articulated in such tableaux as a farmhouse burning brightly in a darkened field, a sunset on the sparkling Mediterranean Sea, and black soldiers and their Caucasian sergeant waiting for a train on the platform at Avignon. To be sure, this pattern of lights and darks contributes to the story's overall design, but, like the symbolic canary itself, they are only part of a carefully orchestrated *metapattern* of oppositions *and* doublings. This complementary system consists of an ontological numbers game in which all the characters participate, and from which they all emerge as losers, as it were, with an aggregate score of zero.

In the opening sequence of "A Canary for One," we're told that the *rapide* "passed very quickly a long, red stone house with a garden," a pleasant prospect that includes the blue Mediterranean and that, as Donaldson suggests, constitutes one half of a binary opposition with "the stifling atmosphere of the train."[1] But in fact the narrator subverts such a binary reading by noticing that the "cutting" which bifurcates the two settings is *also* made of "red stone," like the house, thus blurring any possible bottom line to an either/or interpretation. Such *under*cuttings of strict oppositions are typical of the narrator's complementary habit of mind in "A Canary for One."[2]

The tall negro soldiers and their short white sergeant at Avignon also comprise a binary opposition. A closer reading, however, yields the key addendum: the white sergeant was "with them," a phrase which denotes that the soldiers and their sergeant *also* constitute *one* complementary group or entity.[3] In like manner, the husband and wife who pass them in the train are "with" each other *and* will soon be legally separated; the American lady and her daughter are "with" each other *and* are emotionally distanced; the Swiss engineer and the unhappy daughter will "go on long walks together" in loving memory *and* will remain forever apart, thanks to the American lady's vicious intervention in their lives.

Although they appear strictly oppositional, in fact the details concerning the *maison de couture* in Paris are complementary as well:

> Altogether there had only been these two [*vendeuses*] in twenty years. It had always been the same couturier. Prices, however, had gone up. The exchange, though, equalized that.[4]

Note that the equation here is *not* one *versus* one = two entities, but rather one *minus* one = zero entities. Except for the meaningless substitution of one *vendeuse* by another, nothing of significance happens in the "same" *maison de couture*. What's "equalized" is the symbolic connection between its changeless past and the frozen futures of the American lady and her daughter.

The world of "A Canary for One" is governed by the principle of this zero-based math and by the complementary patterns of ones, twos, and threes that recur throughout the story. Taking these patterns in reverse order, we may begin by noting the matching sets of loveless triangles: the American lady, the wife, and the husband on the train; and the American lady, her daughter, and the Swiss engineer in Vevey. Complementing these triangles are "the three beds from inside the wall" of the sleeping compartment; the three cars in the wreck that confirm the American lady's fears of traveling by *rapide*; the three billboard ads for Belle Jardiniere, Pernot, and Dubonnet near Paris; the Trois Couronnes Hotel in Vevey, where the husband and wife spent their honeymoon; and the three men from Cook's who appear at the Gare de Lyons in Paris.

The narrative is composed of dyadic patternings also. There are, of course, the unhappy pairs of the American husband and wife and the American lady's daughter and the Swiss engineer; the time that has passed ("two years ago this fall") since the American lady took her daughter away from Vevey; "switch-yards and the factory smoke" and "the harbor with stone hills . . . and the last of the sun on the water" in and near Marseilles; the two *vendeuses* from the *maison de couture*; the brown wooden restaurant-cars and brown wooden sleeping-cars on the outskirts of Paris; and the narrator's uncertain "ifs" (". . . if that were the way it were still done"; ". . . if that train still left at five").[5] The dyadic movements of travelers and trains are also noteworthy: "People got on and off"; "the cars . . . went back and forth"; ". . . people in all the seats and the roofs."[6]

It's the number one which, like the *rapide's* "one track" threading through "many others" in the central railyard of Marseilles, serves as a terminal point for the converging affective destinies of the characters.[7] It appears, of course, in the title, where it's noteworthy that a number is substituted for the name of a person. Most commentators assume that the *One* in "A Canary for One" refers solely to the American lady's unhappy daughter in Paris and no one else. But if Hemingway intends for this to be the case, why not assign the girl a name and title the story, say, "A Canary for Susan?" Why does the girl's mother refer to a nameless "very close friend" who castigates foreign men as "some one" in the same breath?[8] Why, for that matter, do most of the "many others" in the story, both present and absent, *share the common characteristic of namelessness?*

A closer look at the two triangles of "A Canary for One" will help to answer these questions. To begin with, in certain respects all three Americans sitting and sleeping on the Paris-bound *rapide* are counterparts. The doubling of husband and wife is obvious: they've fallen out of love with each other and are traveling to Paris

108

to set up separate residences. At no time during the story do they exchange words. Even their farewells to the American lady at the train station in Paris—"my wife said good-by and I said good-by"—are separate but equal.[9] Less obvious is the fact that, in spite of his contempt for her, the narrator and the American lady are also doubles. She is described as being partially deaf, while he reveals at one point that "for several minutes, I had not listened to the American lady".[10] Like her, he is party to a deception involving clothing: he says he wears braces, as opposed to suspenders, to keep up the joking false impression that he is English, not American. For her part, the lady is in the habit of ordering deceptively simple fashions from the expensive *maison de couture* in Paris in order to avoid a luxury tax charged by the post office in America. Finally, the narrator and the lady both show themselves to be past masters of the techniques, both subtle and not so subtle, of eternal sadism. When, knowing full well the lady's pathological fear of derailment, the narrator says, "Look . . . There's been a wreck," he proves himself to be a match for her in cruelty, at least for the moment.[11] The wreckage of the daughter's derailed love affair in Vevey speaks for itself.

The wife too functions as the American lady's counterpart. They both agree that foreign men make poor husbands for American women, and they both identify with memories of the Swiss resort town of Vevey. The American lady, whose fondness for fashion typifies her superficial nature, compliments the wife on her traveling-coat, as if recognizing a kindred spirit. In the second of Hemingway's three typewritten drafts of "A Canary for One," in fact, it's the *wife* who compliments the American lady on what *she* is wearing.[12] Hemingway switched things around at the last minute, fearful, perhaps, that too much of the story's lexical iceberg was showing above the narrative surface. In any event, like her husband, the wife appears to be cut from the same ontological cloth as the American lady.

Best evidence for this may be found in their bittersweet nostalgia for Vevey. According to Joseph DeFalco,

> The word 'love' is a signification of the conflicting elements within the thematic content, and [the] exchange between the wife of the narrator and the American woman points out the irony of the term to those who are themselves estranged from love.[13]

This exchange consists of two sets of complementarities, one positive, the other negative. The positive side of the complementary coin is represented by the noun *love* ("Was the man your daughter was in love with a Swiss?"); the negative side is represented by the adjective *lovely* ("It was a very lovely place").[14] Because an adjective is, in a sense, grammatically estranged from the thing it describes, it's more than fitting that both women should parrot the word *lovely* with reckless and uncaring abandon.

In giving the "ly" to the noun form, in other words, the contra*pun*tal adjective introduces a brittle, cynical tone into the story. Suddenly the women are discussing the pleasures and days of Vevey in the fall and the opulent comforts of the "fine old" Trois Couronnes Hotel.[15] Because they designate roughly the same amount of lexical space for the lush tranquilities of *weather and things* as they do for *people and feelings*, clearly they have both become, as Joseph M. Flora says of the narrator's own waning of affect, "numb" to the emotional demands placed upon them by motherhood and marriage over the years.[16] *See Appendix A.*

Complementarity also governs the relationships in the story's second triangle. Emotionally distanced as they are, the daughter is a budding double for her mother. Like the mother, who is described as "not having slept," the daughter, we are told, "wouldn't sleep at all" following the breakup of her love affair.[17] When the lady adds, "She doesn't care," she may as well be referring to herself as to her daughter.[18]

The fact that the *maison de couture* in Paris "had [the daughter's] measurements"[19] along with those of the mother reinforces the notion that the distanced women function simultaneously as complementary opposites *and* counterparts in the story. As for the young suitor from Vevey, the American lady never indicates whether his plans "to be an engineer" ever came to fruition following the end of the affair. Presumably he was interested in building things (bridges?), whereas the meddlesome mother clearly prefers to tear things—i.e., human relationships—down. On the other hand, the suitor and the mother are both distanced from the ill-starred daughter, one physically, the other emotionally. And, like the married American couple traveling to Paris to set up separate residences, all three are nameless. *See Appendix B.*

The story's two loveless triangles, then, really constitute parallel systems of numbers, wherein, ultimately, $3=2=1=0$. This equation is determined as follows: Three = the three characters in each triangle. Two = the doublings of all three characters in each triangle. One = the "lump sum" of the doublings in each triangle. Complementarity *also* dictates, however, that as long as all three persons are, ontologically speaking, one, the "one" is literally *no one* person. Whether one happens to be a victim, like the American lady's daughter, or a perpetrator, like the mother herself, to suffer the consequences of the denial of love in "A Canary for One" is to become an ontological zero.[20]

As the story's central signifier, the canary "connects" the human angles of its two loveless triangles. Most critics agree with Julian Smith that the canary's entrapment is symbolically mirrored in the walls within walls of the *rapide* and in the American lady's daughter's emotional isolation.[21] Like the canary, the characters—both present and absent—are walled off from each other in different ways. What's gone unnoticed by commentators, however, is the canary's putative self-destructive behavior which, like its imprisoned status, adds a rich symbolic dimension to the story.

The canary's chirping in the morning sunshine is, of course, healthy, normal behavior in domesticated birds. On two occasions, however, the canary *also* pecks into its feathers. This activity is significant if only because Hemingway, the dedicated practitioner of the art of omission in fiction, chooses nonetheless to show it to the reader twice: "The canary shook its feathers and pecked into them." And: ". . . then he dropped his bill and pecked into his feathers again."[22] Feather pecking or picking, far from constituting healthy behavior in caged birds, may be a sign of acute distress. According to the authoritative *The Pet Bird Report*, it occurs in birds which

> have been overprotected and poorly socialized, [and which] may not react well to any new situation, especially if it happens suddenly. If the change directly threatens the bird's sense of security, phobic behavior may result in feather mutilation.

The author goes on to caution that "It is important to protect any young bird from any threatening experience." Symptoms of eating disorders in young birds, she adds, may also include feather pecking.[23]

These descriptions of the causes of pathological behavior in domesticated birds apply with uncanny accuracy to the daughter's psychological profile. Like a distressed bird (and in true complementary fashion) she is at once *over* protected and *under* protected; she, too, is poorly socialized; she, too, has failed to react well to a new situation, namely the sudden destruction of her love affair; she, too, refuses to eat. Therefore, it is the self-mutilating behavior of the canary, not simply its caged status, which mirrors the mutilated psyche of the American lady's daughter.

In lavishing much attention on the controversial last line of "A Canary for One," critics tend to overlook a more significant item: the narrator's inclusion of "one of three men from Cook's" in his account of the journey to Paris. This functionary at the Gare de Lyons also serves as the narrator's counterpart. Like him, the narrator is an anonymous one of three; like him, the narrator doesn't divulge the American lady's name. Most noteworthy of all, like the man from Cook's the narrator *is the caretaker of a text*:

> The porter brought a truck and piled on the baggage, and my wife said good-by and I said good-by to the American lady, whose name had been found by the man from Cook's on a typewritten page in a sheaf of typewritten pages which he replaced in his pocket.[24]

The American lady's name is printed on a typewritten page, only to be stuffed unceremoniously into the pocket of the man from Cook's; we are never permitted to "read" what is written on his travel manifest, namely, the lady's identity.

This omission is consistent with the narrator's own approach to the "typewritten pages" of "A Canary for One." Like the Cook's employee, he is in possession of *and* is possessed by—i.e., is a character in—a text. As we've seen, both texts are characterized by the subtractions of their characters to nameless ontological zeroes. Even their tickets, which are taken by yet another cipher "at the end" of the cement platform and of the story, are consigned to textual oblivion.[25]

Appendix A: *The complementary forms of love*

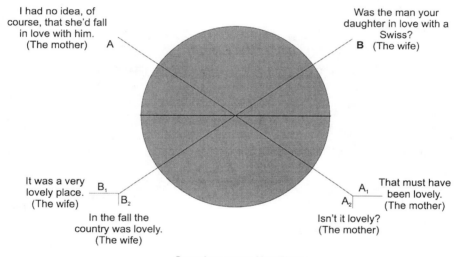

Complementary Positives

My daughter fell in love with a man from Vevey...

I had no idea, of course, that she'd fall in love with him. (The mother)   A

Was the man your daughter in love with a Swiss? **B** (The wife)

It was a very lovely place. B₁ (The wife) |B₂

In the fall the country was lovely. (The wife)

A₁ That must have been lovely. (The mother)

A₂| Isn't it lovely? (The mother)

Complementary Negatives

Appendix B: *The triangles*

3=2=1=0

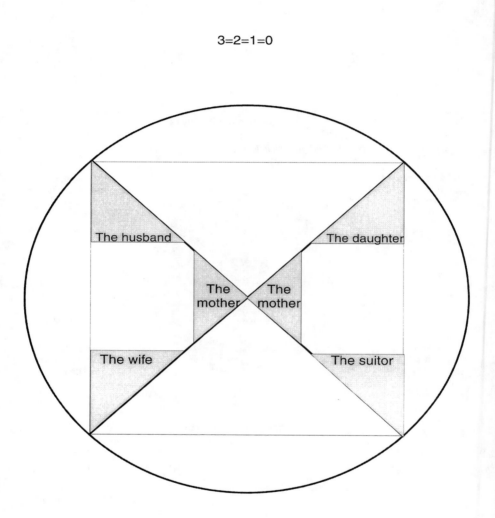

NOTES

1. Scott Donaldson, "Preparing for the End: Hemingway's Revisions of 'A Canary for One,' " in *The Short Stories of Ernest Hemingway: Critical Essays*, ed. Jackson J. Benson (Durham: Duke University Press, 1975), p. 231.

2. Ernest Hemingway, *The Short Stories of Ernest Hemingway* (New York: Scribners, 1938), p. 337.

3. *Ibid.*, p. 338.

4. *Ibid.*, p. 340.

5. *Ibid.*, p. 340.

6. *Ibid.*, pp. 338, 340.

7. *Ibid.*, p. 337.

8. *Ibid.*, p. 339.

9. *Ibid.*, p. 341.

Complementarity requires, of course, that the situations of the husband and wife be examined from a reverse angle as well. Evidence in the story also points to faint but perceptible traces of caring on the part of both. Of the husband, for instance, Joseph DeFalco writes,

> A little earlier in the narrative he [notes] a farmhouse burning. It is obvious that [such] details are direct referents to his own situation, but what they also imply is a value judgment on his part. Marital estrangement means a literal wrecking or burning of a relationship and a consequent ruin of the normal course of life. Love-relationships must be cared for in much the same fashion as a canary (*The Hero in Hemingway's Short Stories* [Pittsburgh: University of Pittsburgh Press, 1963], pp. 175-76).

As for the wife, Trisha Ingman suggests that she, too, hasn't wholly succeeded in denying her feelings. What's done is done, but not without a hint of regret:

> After [the American woman] tells about having taken her daughter away from the man she loved, the wife's first question is, "Did she get over it?" The American woman's reply is, "I don't think so." The inquiry can be seen as one about her own future as well as about the daughter's past. The wife is still in love with her husband; it's not likely that she will get over the separation soon ("Symbolic Motifs in 'A Canary for One'," *Linguistics in Literature* 1 [1976]: 36).

10. Hemingway, *The Short Stories of Ernest Hemingway*, p. 339.

11. *Ibid.*, p. 341.

12. Donaldson, "Preparing for the End: Hemingway's Revisions of 'A Canary for One,' " p. 233.

13. DeFalco, *The Hero in Hemingway's Short Stories*, p. 175.

14. Hemingway, *The Short Stories of Ernest Hemingway*, p. 339.

15. *Ibid.*, pp. 339-41.

16. Joseph M. Flora, *Ernest Hemingway: A Study of the Short Fiction* (Boston: Twayne Publishers, 1989), p. 39.

17. Hemingway, *The Short Stories of Ernest Hemingway*, pp. 338, 339.

18. *Ibid.*, p. 339.

19. *Ibid.*, p. 340.

20. At journey's end the narrator comes out with a curious observation: "Nothing had eaten any breakfast" (Hemingway, *The Short Stories of Ernest Hemingway*, p. 340). Since he, too, has apparently gone without the morning meal, the remark indicates that he is at least subliminally aware of his ontological status as, literally, a "hollow man."

21. *Ibid.*, p. 359.

22. *Ibid.*, p. 339.

23. Sally Blanchard, "The Complexities of Feather Picking," *The Pet Bird Report* 5 (1995): 12.

24. Hemingway, *The Short Stories of Ernest Hemingway*, p. 341.

25. *Ibid.*, p. 342.

Krebs's Zero Summer: "Soldier's Home"

> Where is the summer, the unimaginable
> Zero Summer?
> —*Little Gidding*

> In this way he lost everything.
> —*Soldier's Home*

Oftentimes the protagonists of Hemingway's short stories are avid readers of texts. In "The Three-Day Blow," the adolescents Nick and Bill carry on a solemn literary discussion about the relative merits of G.K. Chesterton and George Meredith; the indifferent husband of "Cat in the Rain" buries his nose in a book in order to fend off the demands of his frustrated wife; the father in "A Day's Wait" reads Howard Pyle's *Book of Pirates* out loud to Schatz, the nine-year-old boy who's convinced that he's dying; the insular Mrs. Adams in "The Doctor and the Doctor's Wife" is a devotee of *Science and Health with Key to the Scriptures* by Mary Baker Eddy (her husband, on the other hand, is defined by an unopened pile of medical journals sitting on the floor of his room). And so forth.

Krebs, the deracinated veteran of "Soldier's Home," is also a bookworm. Having returned to Oklahoma following his participation in the First World War, he is in the habit of leaving the house on lazy summer mornings "to walk down town to the library to get a book."[1] In one significant respect, however, Krebs's reading habits differ from those of his aforementioned counterparts in the Hemingway canon—he is also a putative character in the book Hemingway assigns to him:

> He sat there on the porch reading a book on the war. It was a history
> and he was reading about all the engagements he had been in. It was
> the most interesting reading he had ever done.

The problem is, of course, that Krebs can't locate his soldier-self in his favorite text:

> He wished there were more maps. He looked forward with a good feeling to reading all the really good histories when they would come out with good detail maps. Now he was really learning about the war. He had been a good soldier.[2]

A classic American fictional archetype, Harold Krebs is the quintessential displaced or missing person—Washington Irving's Rip Van Winkle, Herman Melville's Ishmael, and Mark Twain's Huckleberry Finn come immediately to mind—who is eternally suspended between memory and desire, wanderlust and nostalgia, the past and the future. Krebs's *ontological* state of suspense is duplicated by a state of *lexical* suspense which Hemingway induces in his readers. This reflexivity or *rapprochement* between text and reader is articulated in twofold fashion: as semiology and as structure.

I

As a point of departure, I'd like to propose "A Simple Inquiry," a story of the war that Harold Krebs in "Soldier's Home" has left far behind. Both of these stories have one thing in common: they both lend themselves, in part, to semiotic analysis.

Of "A Simple Enquiry," Gerry Brenner has written:

> The map on the pine-board wall, the room's only 'decoration,' signifies that *map-reading* is important to what the men in the hut engage in. The papers on which the major and his clerk work signify that *paper-reading* is also important—as is *book-reading* to the clerk. . . . When the major challenges Pinin's admission that he is in love with a girl. . . . it becomes clear that *letter-reading* is also significant to the officer and his clerk.[3]

Both "Soldier's Home" and "A Simple Enquiry" contain what Brenner calls "semantic riddles" which problematize the act of reading and which, therefore, include as subject matter the reader's search for meaning. Interestingly, the semantic riddles in both stories are articulated by the same four signs: maps, "papers," books, and letters. The functions of these signs are diametrically opposed to each other, however, in the two works.

To begin with, the military map on the pine-board wall of "A Simple Enquiry" is missing from "Soldier's Home" because, as Krebs discovers to his chagrin, maps have not yet been included in the freshly-written history books of World War I. In like manner, the "paper-reading" of "A Simple Enquiry," which takes up the time of both the major and the adjutant Tonani, comes under erasure in "Soldier's Home." Krebs's mother implores him over breakfast, "[P]lease don't muss up the paper," adding that if the morning *Star* is mussed, the (always absent) father will not read it. Then, because his mother also demands his undivided attention, Krebs is obliged to "put down the paper," thus negating another escape into a world of signs.[4]

In "A Simple Enquiry," the busy clerk Tonani is in possession of a "paper-covered" book.[5] On the contrary, the lackadaisical Harold Krebs must look forward to the "really good histories" of World War I that have yet to be written.[6] Balancing these missing definitive histories of the Great War is Krebs's mother's passing reference to the history of another war: the lurid stories told by her father of the American Civil War. We don't know what these stories were, nor, for that matter, do we have any way of knowing if they are true.

The reading habits of the inquisitive major of a "A Simple Enquiry" aren't merely restricted to maps and papers: "I read all your letters," he informs Pinin.[7] In contrast, the mail that Krebs's sister Helen brings to the breakfast table in "Soldier's

Home" is never opened. Here, too, Krebs and the reader are denied access to a text or texts.

The semiotic inversions of "Soldier's Home" also extend to character and setting. Four *dramatis personae* are missing from the story: Krebs's grandfather who fought in the Civil War; his second, unnamed sister; Charley Simmons, the "credit to the community" held up to Krebs by his mother; and, of course, the "non-committal" father who spends all of his allotted time in the story at work.[8] Omissions and disappearances characterize the story's settings as well. The conspicuous absence of the Rhine River from a photograph taken "on the Rhine" has been noted by many critics; Krebs declares himself to be AWOL from God's Kingdom, an admission that causes his mother grief; and Krebs's decision not to confront the missing father is accompanied by the antistrophe, "He would miss that one."[9]

These and the other aforementioned omissions in the story serve to conscript both Krebs *and* the reader in a quest for missing persons, places, or things. A fresh look at the structure of "Soldier's Home" will also help to elucidate the role Hemingway has prepared for the protagonist and the reader in this ongoing quest.

II

Much critical scrutiny has been devoted to Hemingway's intricate strategy of patterning in "Soldier's Home." Of the "loaded" references to sports in the story, for instance, Robert W. Lewis, Jr. has written,

> In this story of a returned Marine veteran of World War I, sport as such seems incidental to what first appears as a casually ironic recounting of the trials of a veteran's readjustment to civilian life. But each detail is loaded, and the few references to sport—to pool, motoring, reading the sporting page of the newspaper, and girls'

'indoor baseball'— . . . form an important pattern of their own in this story about patterns.[10]

Kenneth G. Johnston has also noticed the importance of patterns in "Soldier's Home," pointing out that Krebs himself thinks in terms of patterns.[11] According to Johnston, Krebs's chief desire is to attain

> a smooth uncomplicated life in a world of patterns and colliding forces. When the patterns or collisions are simple, predictable, and impersonal, such as a game of pool or baseball, he can enjoy the situation. It is the sporting page that he reads at breakfast. But when the situation involves a collision of values, personalities, and attitudes, as in a family quarrel; or a social pattern of conformity, lies, and restraint, as in courtship; he would rather escape into the 'cool dark of the pool room' or into a book.[12]

Like Lewis, Johnston interprets the patterns of "Soldier's Home" strictly in terms of *repetition*. For Lewis, the story is "written in a wonderfully ironic, carefully modulated style in which Hemingway is in full control of verbal repetition and variations on his theme."[13] For Johnston, the verbal "pattern of repetition" which toolmarks one section of the story "reflects upon the repetitive pattern of the courtship ritual, of the courtship lies" which permeates "Soldier's Home" as a whole.[14] Both Lewis and Johnston commit the same serious error of omission: in pointing to the story's discrete patterns of repetition, they fail to recognize the *anti-patterns* that accompany them. Neither leading critic of "Soldier's Home," that is to say, acknowledges the presence of complementarity as the story's pivotal structural device.

Johnston sees the following repetitions as cut from whole lexical cloth: *want . . . did not want . . . want . . . did not want . . .* In similar fashion, Lewis describes the phrases, *before the war . . . after the war. . .* in terms of *one* reiterative system. These interpretations are helpful, but they fail to account for the *anti*-patterns of which the story's narrative refrains are also constituted. These patterns and anti-patterns in "Soldier's Home" are not binary; they are designed, rather, to *share equal billing as fictions*. The patternings of reality in the story are not strictly repetitive *or* contradictory, but complementary; as the narrator says of Krebs's dilemma, "It was all a lie both ways."[15]

Put another way, the worlds of war and peace in "Soldier's Home" are depicted as being at once identical *and* oppositional, with Harold Krebs trapped in an ontological twilight zone in between. It's certainly true that Krebs's experience then (in France and Germany) and now (at home) is characterized by doublings; as many critics have noted, in a college photo taken before the War he and his fraternity brothers wear "exactly the same height and style collar," while as an ex-soldier he admires the "round Dutch collars" worn by local girls.[16] On the other hand, even though his father's car is also doubled—the narrator refers to it as "still the same car" as before the War—Krebs's association with it past and future is strictly oppositional.[17] While his parents are now willing to let him "take [the car] out in the evenings," he wasn't allowed to do so before enlisting in the Marines.[18]

Krebs's romantic interests before and after the War are also depicted in oppositional terms. Although the German girls in a War photo "are not beautiful," his home town is replete with "so many good-looking young girls" whom Krebs "liked to look at."[19] Nonetheless, when Krebs contemplates the complicated world of the pretty girls of his home town, he unconsciously uses the terms routinely used by historians to describe the Great War. For both soldier and scholars, conflicts between nations and town girls amount to the same thing: "already defined alliances and shifting feuds."[20] When Krebs attends a dance, he "fell into the easy pose of the old soldier among other soldiers."[21] Elsewhere, he reflects that "it was all right to pose as though you had to have a girl," a trick he learned *in the army*.[22] When Krebs lies about the horrors of warfare to friends, he "acquired the nausea in regard to experience that is the result of untruth or exaggeration," a feeling that is reprised during the story's terrible last scene, when, upon lying to his mother about loving her, he "felt sick and vaguely nauseated."[23]

Consider too the acute interest of Krebs's male acquaintances in second-hand stories of helpless German women chained to machine guns in the Argonne forest. Interestingly, when Krebs's "quite unimportant" lies don't measure up to this sensational scuttlebutt, his friends lose interest in both them and in Krebs himself.[24] As we've seen, these lurid stories *may* be matched in sensationalism by Krebs's grandfather's tales of the Civil War, tales which—in Krebs's mother's view—reveal the weakness of men, even as the tales from the Argonne woods reveal women as the weaker sex.

In fact, Mrs. Krebs's contempt for men helps to explain why Krebs's male friends are so fascinated by the notion of German women in chains. For it turns out that American men are *also* chained, not to machine guns, but to matriarchal custom. Depicted by the titillated young men as slaves in war, the women of "Soldier's Home" are also depicted as masters in peacetime. Krebs's sister insists that she can "pitch better than lots of the boys"; his mother is fond of reminding him "how weak men are"; and Krebs himself acknowledges his mother's power when he says, "I'll bet you made him," referring to his father's decision to let him drive the car.[25]

We have no way of knowing, however, whether or not young Helen is boasting or telling the truth; we cannot know if Krebs's mother is right, since she obviously has many axes to grind, among them her religious beliefs; nor will we ever learn if Krebs wins his bet, since the father never appears in the story. Once again, the oppositional positives and negatives of war and peace in "Soldier's Home" double as complementary fictions.

In "Soldier's Home," these fictions take the supreme form of emotional blackmail. In response to the prodding of his favorite sister Helen, Krebs declares that he'll love her "always." But when he waffles about watching her play indoor baseball, she accuses him of making up a fiction: "Aw, Hare, you don't love me."[26] This fiction comes to life a moment later, when his mother takes over, as it were, for Helen:

> "Don't you love your mother, dear boy?"
> "No," Krebs said.[27]

If Krebs's waffling disappoints his sister, his plain talk utterly shatters the mother. In complementary fashion, however, *the truth becomes a fiction again*, as Krebs adds resignedly, "I didn't mean I didn't love you."[28]

Here and elsewhere, Krebs's fatal flaw is his failure to understand the story's central irony: he is, in fact, *living in a text*, one that he cannot read, even as the other texts in "Soldier's Home" are missing for him and for the reader. Krebs's own observation early on, "The world they [the town girls] were in was not the world he was in," rests on a false premise that reflects his binary habit of mind throughout the story, namely that the world of innocence is false and the world of experience is real.[29] It's precisely because Krebs is unaware that his *idée reçu* of a dichotomy between fact and fiction is *itself* a falsehood that the reader must, as John Unterecker says of W.B. Yeats's "Lapis Lazuli," "bolt [the form] together into final shape."[30] In doing so, he is thereby conscripted by Hemingway's narratology into conjoining semiology and structure into a virtually seamless whole: a lexical complementary system.

NOTES

1. Ernest Hemingway, *The Short Stories of Ernest Hemingway* (New York: Scribners, 1938), p. 146.

2. *Ibid.*, p. 148.

3. Gerry Brenner, "A Semiotic Inquiry into Hemingway's 'A Simple Enquiry,' " in *Hemingway's Neglected Short Fiction: New Perspectives,* ed. Susan F. Beegel (Tuscaloosa: University of Alabama Press, 1989), pp. 198-99.

4. Hemingway, *The Short Stories of Ernest Hemingway*, pp. 149-50.

5. *Ibid.*, p. 327.

6. *Ibid.*, p. 148.

7. *Ibid.*, p. 329.

8. *Ibid.*, pp. 151, 146.

9. *Ibid*, pp. 145, 153.

10. Robert W. Lewis, "Hemingway's Concept of Sport and 'Soldier's Home,' " in *The Short Stories of Ernest Hemingway: Critical Essays*, ed. Jackson J. Benson (Durham: Duke University Press, 1975), p. 175.

11. Kenneth G. Johnston, *The Tip of the Iceberg: Hemingway and the Short Story* (Greenwood, Fla.: The Penkeville Publishing Co., 1987), p. 79.

12. *Ibid.*, p. 79.

13. Lewis, "Hemingway's Concept of Sport and 'Soldier's Home,' " p. 174.

14. Johnston, *The Tip of the Iceberg*, p. 79.

15. *Ibid.*, p. 148.

16. Hemingway, *The Short Stories of Ernest Hemingway*, pp. 145, 147.

17. *Ibid.*, p. 147.

18. *Ibid.*, p. 149.

19. *Ibid.*, pp. 146, 147.

20. *Ibid.*, p. 147.

21. *Ibid.*, p. 146.

22.   *Ibid.*, p. 147.

23.   *Ibid.*, p. 152.

24.   *Ibid.*, p. 146.

25.   *Ibid.*, pp. 150, 151, 149.

26.   *Ibid.,* p. 150.

27.   *Ibid.*, pp. 151-152.

28.   *Ibid.*, p. 152.

29.   *Ibid.*, p. 148.

30.   John Unterecker, *A Reader's Guide to William Butler Yeats* (New York: The Noonday Press, 1959), p. 258.

The Odd Couples:
"The Sea Change" and "Hills Like White Elephants"

I

F rom several vantages, "The Sea Change" and "Hills Like White Elephants" seem very different stories. One takes place in France, the other in Spain; one is set indoors, the other (mostly) outdoors; one deals with homosexual, the other with heterosexual love or desire; one features an incipient abortion, the other an incipient abandonment; the action in one story is initiated by a man, in the other by a woman; the couple in "Hills" will more than likely stay together, in "Sea" they separate; and so forth. As Sheldon Norman Grebstein has shown, however, the two short narratives also have a great deal in common:

> In "Hills Like White Elephants" and "The Sea Change" dialogue is not only essential, it is the totality. No external plot remains; the situation has been condensed to people talking. . . . [A]lthough the dialogue compresses the entire relationship of the characters into a single brief conversation, it supplies enough evidence to enable us to reconstruct the past.[1]

J. Bakker extends Grebstein's claims, arguing that "Hills" and "Sea" correspond "strongly in form and in theme," although for Bakker "the dialogue of 'The Sea Change' is much weaker and far less dramatic than that of 'Hills.' "[2]

While Bakker is correct to insist that the two stories resemble each other formally and thematically (his critique of the dialogue in "The Sea Change," on the other hand, is debatable), neither he nor Grebstein discusses the similarities or the differences between them in sufficient detail.[3] In the reading(s) which I'll propose, both the differences *and* the similarities between "Hills Like White Elephants" and "The Sea Change" must be taken into account if we are to understand them—as I believe Hemingway meant us to—as a single lexical unit: a *complementary metanarrative.*

If we hold a written text to a mirror, we see what H.H. Pattee has called "a paradoxical articulation": the words are at once reflected and reversed.[4] When held up to "Hills Like White Elephants" and "The Sea Change," this dyadic principle of mirroring reveals that each narrative comprises the opposite side of the same complementary coin. Male *and* female, heterosexual *and* homosexual, all four characters in "Sea" and "Hills" transcend the binary logic of gender politics by performing a fourfold tragic ritual whose outcome is not merely the end of this or that romantic relationship, but the virtual annihilation of the social self of each participant.

It's a critical commonplace that the central agitation in stories like "The Sea Change" and "Hills Like White Elephants" derives from that ubiquitous *bête blanche* of Hemingway criticism, the thing left out. In "Sea," we never meet the putative lesbian lover; at the conclusion of "Hills," the "simple operation"—i.e., the abortion—is yet to be performed. But when we read these stories as chapters in an interconnected *historia calamitatum*, we discover that these omitted yet pivotal situations—both of which threaten to destroy the relationship between the man and the woman in each story—also function dyadically: when each story is held up to the other like a mirror, the women's and the men's roles are both reflected and reversed in precise fashion. Viewing these narratives from a complementary perspective enables us to see Hemingway's version(s) of the battle of the sexes in a new light.

To begin with, both men—Phil in "The Sea Change" and the unnamed American lover in "Hills"—want to destroy "the thing left out." Phil in "Sea" threatens to "kill her"—his lesbian rival—while Jig's companion in "Hills" wants her to permit an abortionist to "let the air in," terminating the life of their unborn child.[5] Both men are closet rationalists, relying as they do on proof as a bargaining chip. From "Sea":

> "Don't you really believe I love you?"
> "Why don't you prove it?"
> "You never used to talk that way. You never asked me to prove anything. That isn't polite."[6]

From "Hills":

> "They look like white elephants," she said.
> "I've never seen one," the man drank his beer.
> "No, you wouldn't have."
> "I might have," the man said. "Just because you say I wouldn't have doesn't prove anything."[7]

In addition, Hemingway applies the so-called Uncle Charles Principle of narrative poetics to the two men only.[8] In "Hills," the American looks at the people waiting "reasonably" for the train— "reasonably," as is often noted, is precisely the word this particular character (as opposed to the narrator) would use, since his sole purpose in life appears to be to persuade Jig to be "logical" and have the abortion (as if reason, not emotion, were the only issue involved).[9] And at the conclusion of "Sea," the narrator declares that Phil was "really quite a different-looking man," an echo of Phil's own remark to the barman of a moment before, "You see in me quite a different man."[10]

The women in the stories, too, share significant features. Neither wants "the thing left out" mentioned—the girl in "Sea" says, "You don't have to put any name to it," while Jig in "Hills" is mute on the delicate subject of abortion ("The girl did not say anything").[11] Both *appear* to be happy in their respective

dénouements—"There's nothing wrong with me. I feel fine," Jig says in "Hills";
"You're too good to me," the woman tells Phil in "Sea."[12] But Hemingway has
planted seeds of doubt in both instances. Jig will suffer from remorse, while Phil's
lover insists that she'll return to him, suggesting at least that her future fling with the
lesbian lover will indeed be superficially sensual.

In part, "The Sea Change" and "Hills Like White Elephants" are about the
creation of fictions. These fictions—which open on to a series of dyadic oppositions
counterbalancing the doublings outlined above—are authored by the unnamed
woman in "Sea" and by the unnamed man in "Hills." The crux of fiction-making in
"Sea" is the woman's protestory remark, "I love you very much"; in "Hills," the crux
is the man's equally protestory, "You know I love you," and "I don't want you to do
it . . . [i.e., have the abortion]."[13] These statements are, of course, in direct opposition
to the speakers' true intentions, motivations, and/or feelings (this is especially the
case with the American in "Hills").

Other oppositions may be stated in brief, as follows. The man in "Sea" is
given a name; in "Hills," the woman is named. In "Sea," Phil prefers to turn a deaf
ear to the girl ("I'd rather not hear"); in "Hills," Jig asks the man to "please . . . stop
talking."[14] Of greater significance are the dynamics of the central conflict in each
story. From the male point of view in "Hills," the abortion is "perfectly natural";
from Jig's perspective, it is unnatural.[15] On the other hand, from Phil's perspective
in "Sea," the lesbian affair is clearly unnatural, while from his lover's vantage the
affair is not only natural, it's what she earnestly desires (Jig, on the other hand,
doesn't want to abort her baby).

The key issue of trust is forced by the man in "Hills" ("We can have
everything") and by the woman in "Sea" ("Don't you trust me?").[16] Gestures toward
religion are made by Phil in "Sea"—"I swear to God," and "I wish to God . . .," and

by Jig in "Hills," who "put her hand out and took hold of two of the strings of beads," as if the bead curtain in the railway station cafe were a Catholic rosary.[17] In "Sea," a *male* service person—James the barman—functions as a dramatic device designed to reveal Phil's disintegrating sense of self. As Warren Bennett has convincingly argued, the men are counterparts:

> [Phil's] standing at the bar with male prostitutes, as is James (the barman) marks the end of everything. . . . and just as the girl has called him 'old Phil,' the two homosexuals call the barman 'old James.'[18]

In "Hills," however, a *female* service person subtly serves as the revelatory male counterpart. Both characters use the same words: "Do you want it [i.e., the Anis del Toro] with water?" (the American to Jig); "You want them with water?" (the barwoman to the American).[19] As is the case in "Sea," the purpose of this doubling is to reveal a hidden, unpleasant truth about the male protagonist, namely, that the American has control of the situation because he speaks Spanish.

The most telling complementary opposition between the two sets of characters lies in the dénouement to each narrative. In "Sea," the man is the apparent loser: "He watched her go. He was not the same-looking man as he had been before he told her to go."[20] In "Hills," of course, Jig is the one who—once she goes through with the abortion—will never be "the same." Nevertheless, even though it appears that the woman in "Sea" and the man in "Hills" will win their internecine battles by obtaining the thing that they most desire, they've all but sacrificed their humanity—their capacity for caring, even their ability to love—in the process.

For both "Sea" and "Hills" "stress the interdependence, however unhappy, between the sexes," as Rena Sanderson has written of Hemingway's short fiction in general.[21] Giving gender complementarity the critical attention it so rarely receives, Sanderson adds, helps to demolish "another common but mistaken assumption about Hemingway's fiction," the notion that "Hemingway automatically sides with his fictional males."[22] The best way to avoid this sort of clichéd diegesis of stories like "The Sea Change" and "Hills Like White Elephants" is to eschew altogether the binary logic of either/or, male vs. female, and victim vs. oppressor. On the contrary, a complementary reading (i.e., one which embraces the alternative logic of both/and) clearly reveals that *all* four characters—Phil in "Sea," Jig in "Hills," and their unnamed companions—are losers in the evenly matched guerrilla wars of love that characterize many of Hemingway's least-understood short fictions.

II

Gender transposition is a technique that critics have traditionally ascribed to latter-day novels by Hemingway like *Islands in the Stream* and *The Garden of Eden.*[23] A poetics of complementarity indicates, however, that gender transposition also occurs in earlier short works like "Hills Like White Elephants" and "The Sea Change." According to the dyadic principle of mirroring, the put-upon Phil in "The Sea Change" is the clear counterpart of Jig in "Hills Like White Elephants," while the dominant unnamed woman in "Sea" plays a role equivalent to the dominant unnamed man in "Hills." In spite of her lackluster attempt at sarcasm ("And I'll do it and then everything will be fine") Jig will probably have the abortion, while Phil almost certainly intends to "forgive" the girl ("And when you come back tell me all about it").[24]

However, complementarity also dictates that this is (literally) only half the story. In "Sea," James, the white-faced, white-jacketed barman, points the way to the girl's probable future:

He knew these two and thought them a handsome young couple. He had seen many handsome couples break up *and new couples form that were never so handsome long.* (italics added)[25]

The suggestion here is that the "new" lesbian couple will not stay together for long either, which perhaps explains why the girl tries to hedge her bets: "I'll come back . . . Of course I will."[26]

Warren Bennett is correct, therefore, to point out that from the girl's point of view "a sexual act is a sexual act, whether it is heterosexual or homosexual. The act cannot be judged in terms of gender." Bennett also emphasizes the gender-neutral connotations of the girl's remarks to Phil: "We're made up of all sorts of things," and, "You've known that. You've used it well enough."[27]

But in emphasizing Phil's total sexual humiliation, Bennett fails to see that the girl is probably no better off than he is, and that the overriding issue here is not the triumph of sex but the failure of love. In both stories, the pursuit of freewheeling, gratuitous lovemaking carries with it emotional consequences that no one, male *or* female, is morally equipped to deal with. Joseph DeFalco is nearer the mark:

. . . 'The Sea Change' does reveal something important about the nature of *man*. Most of Hemingway's fiction conforms to Pope's dictum to study man, and Hemingway over and over grounds his materials in humanity. . . . Most of man's difficulties are based on his own failings, making him *both victim and conspirator.*

"Hemingway's focus upon the normal or upon the abnormal makes little difference," DeFalco adds, "for the portrayal of individuals working out their separate destinies usually encompasses both" (italics added).[28]

Although DeFalco has "The Sea Change" specifically in mind, his observations are equally applicable to "Hills Like White Elephants." From an even broader perspective, both genders in both stories may be said to conform to Baudelaire's universal axiom for the canker hidden at the heart of all romantic relationships:

> I believe that I have set down in my notes that Love greatly resembles an application of torture or a surgical operation. . . . For even when two lovers love passionately and are full of mutual desire, one of the two will always be cooler and less self-abandoned than the other. He or she is the surgeon, or executioner; the other, the patient, or victim.[29]

A final word on Jig in "Hills Like White Elephants." As she gazes across the fertile fields "along the banks of the Ebro," she murmurs, "'And we could have all this. . . . [W]e could have everything.' "[30] At this poignant moment in the story, she appears at her most vulnerable and sympathetic. As commentators have recognized from the start, the moral status of her lover is clear enough: he's as cold and unfeeling as any protagonist in Hemingway's short fiction—as Jim Gilmore in "Up in Michigan," for instance (only the bestial narrator of "After the Storm" surpasses him in sheer inhumanity). When Jig looks wistfully at the elegiac shadow of a cloud that "moved across the field of grain" near the Ebro, she seems a perfect foil for her indifferent American companion.[31]

But Jig is hardly an innocent bystander in what has happened to them and what is apparently about to happen to her. Even though it's her lover who gazes not at the river and the trees but at the "labels on [the bags] from all the hotels where they had spent nights," we should keep in mind that the bags contain Jig's belongings as well as his.[32] But Jig's true Achilles heel comes in the form of uncaringness, the moral disease that afflicts all four protagonists in "The Sea Change" and "Hills Like White Elephants":

"Then I'll do it. Because I don't care about me."
"What do you mean?"
"I don't care about me."
"Well, I care about you."[33]

If Jig's lover is revealed in this exchange as a hypocrite, Jig herself is revealed at the very least as a narcissist who, in not caring about "me," conveniently forgets that it is *another being*, namely her own child, who is about to be sacrificed.[34] Once again, Hemingway refuses to take sides in the wars of love. Once again, we are presented with what Edwin J. Barton calls portraits of "highly complex, fluid, and dynamic relations between the sexes" in stories like "'Out of Season,' 'Hills Like White Elephants,' and 'The Sea Change.'" In these particular works, Barton astutely adds, "the stories of *eros tyrannos* are rarely just what we would expect."[35]

"Hills" was published in *Men Without Women* in 1927, while "Sea" appeared in *Winner Take Nothing* in 1933. The complementary features of "Hills" and "Sea," however, recall a third Hemingway short story: "Mr. and Mrs. Elliot," which had already appeared in *In Our Time* back in 1924. Interestingly, and perhaps not fortuitously, the plot of "Mr. and Mrs. Elliot" may be interpreted as a dress rehearsal for its two successors—a sort of proto-metanarrative.

In contrast to Jig and the American in "Hills Like White Elephants," the couple in "Mr. and Mrs. Elliot" are more than amenable to the idea of childbirth:

Mr. and Mrs. Elliot tried very hard to have a baby. They tried as often as Mrs. Elliot could stand it. They tried in Boston after they were married and they tried coming over on the boat.[36]

And *contra* the angry Phil in "The Sea Change" ("I'll kill her"), the effete Mr. Elliott countenances a lesbian relationship between his wife and another woman:

136

> Mrs. Elliot and the girl friend now slept together in the big medieval bed. They had many a good cry together. In the evening they all sat at dinner together in the garden under a plane tree and the hot evening wind blew and Elliot drank white wine and Mrs. Elliot and the girl friend made conversation and they were all quite happy.[37]

The three stories are also conjoined, however, by the complementary thematic thread of narcissism. In "Mr. and Mrs. Elliot," upon seeing "all the pairs of shoes" outside the rooms of a Boston Hotel, the sexually excited husband "hurried back to his own room," only to find his wife sound asleep. No matter: "He did not like to waken her and soon everything was quite all right and he slept peacefully."[38] After Mrs. Elliot takes up with her lesbian lover, the onanistic Mr. Elliot keeps to his own room where he writes poetry at night, only to emerge in the morning looking "very exhausted."[39] The "very" leaves little to the reader's imagination as to what else Mr. Elliot has been doing behind closed doors. In spilling the seed that might have produced a child— "soon everything was quite all right"—Mr. Elliot complements the conditions of the men and women in "The Sea Change" and "Hills Like White Elephants." Like him, all of them appear doomed to kill the thing they love.

NOTES

1.   Sheldon Norman Grebstein, *Hemingway's Craft* (Carbondale: Southern Illinois University Press, 1973), p. 111.

2.   J. Bakker, *Ernest Hemingway: The Artist as Man of Action* (Assan, N.V.: Van Gorcum & Company, 1972), p. 144.

3.   Joseph M. Flora joins Grebstein and Bakker in drawing brief connections between the stories, pointing out that the narrators' references to the females in both narratives as "the 'girl' . . . tends to make the woman more vulnerable" (Joseph M. Flora, *Ernest Hemingway: A Study of the Short Fiction* [Boston: Twayne Publishers, 1989], p. 66). Flora's otherwise astute observation suffers from the same implicit short-sightedness shared by commentators of Hemingway's fiction who insist that men are generally the aggressors, if not always the victors, in the war between the sexes. A complementary reading of short stories like "The Sea Change" and "Hills Like White Elephants" calls into question such binary assumptions.

4.   H.H. Pattee, "The Complementarity Principle in Biological and Social Structures," *Journal of Social and Biological Structures* I (April 1978): 192.

5.   Ernest Hemingway, *The Short Stories of Ernest Hemingway* (New York: Scribners, 1938), pp. 397, 275.

6.   *Ibid.*, p. 398.

7.   *Ibid.*, p. 273.

8.   The "Uncle Charles Principle," where the third-person narrator adopts the speech patterns and/or the idioms of a character, is often associated with the work of James Joyce, from whom Hemingway almost certainly learned it. For a thoroughgoing discussion of this technique, see Hugh Kenner, *Joyce's Voices* (Berkeley: University of California Press, 1978).

9.   Hemingway, *The Short Stories of Ernest Hemingway*, p. 278.

10.   *Ibid.*, p. 401.

11.   *Ibid.*, pp. 400, 275.

12.   *Ibid.*, pp. 278, 400.

13.   *Ibid.*, pp. 398, 275, 277.

14.   *Ibid.*, pp. 398, 277.

15.   *Ibid.*, p. 275.

16.   *Ibid.*, pp. 276, 398.

17.   *Ibid.*, pp. 397, 275.

        The first critic to make the connection between the curtain beads and the Roman Catholic
        rosary was Gary D. Elliott. See "Hemingway's 'Hills Like White Elephants,' " *The
        Explicator* 35 (1977): 22-23.

18.   Warren Bennett, " 'That's Not Very Polite': Sexual Identity in Hemingway's 'The
        Sea Change,' " in *Hemingway's Neglected Short Fiction: New Perspectives*, ed. Susan
        F. Beegel (Tuscaloosa: University of Alabama Press, 1989), p. 241.

19.   Hemingway, *The Short Stories of Ernest Hemingway*, p. 274.

20.   *Ibid.*, pp. 400-01.

21.   Rena Sanderson, "Hemingway and Gender History," in *The Cambridge Companion to
        Hemingway*, ed. Scott Donaldson (New York: Cambridge University Press, 1996), p.
        176.

22.   *Ibid.*, p. 176.

23.   The ambiguous or androgynous sexuality that toolmarks these two posthumous works
        has been well-documented by critics. Susan F. Beegel points out, however, that "such
        themes" as "male androgyny, bisexuality, and lesbianism . . . are omnipresent in the work
        published during Hemingway's lifetime" (Susan F. Beegel, "The Critical Reputation of
        Ernest Hemingway," in *The Cambridge Companion to Hemingway*, p. 290). Rena
        Sanderson detects the technique of gender transposition in the longer fictions as far back
        as *The Sun Also Rises*:

                . . . Brett resembles a traditional man in her sexual
                expectations, and Jake resembles a traditional woman in his
                sexual unavailability and his uncomplaining tolerance of
                others' inconsiderations. The reversal, both overt and
                implied, in their gender roles signals that something has gone
                awry between the sexes. (Sanderson, "Hemingway and
                Gender History," p. 179.)

24.   Hemingway, *The Short Stories of Ernest Hemingway*, pp. 276, 400.

25.   *Ibid.*, p. 399.

26.   *Ibid.*, p. 400.

27.   *Ibid.*, p. 400.

28.   Joseph DeFalco, *The Hero in Hemingway's Short Stories* (Pittsburgh: University of
        Pittsburgh Press, 1963), p. 161.

29.   *Ibid.*, p. 161.

30.   Hemingway, *The Short Stories of Ernest Hemingway*, p. 276.

31.   *Ibid.*, p. 276.

32.   *Ibid.*, p. 277.

33.   *Ibid.*, pp. 276-77.

34.   From the perspective of "gender-based linguistics," Pamela Smiley also demonstrates that the relationship between Jig and her lover is complementary, one of both/and, as opposed to either/or:

> As a result of these differences [in speech patterns], there are two Jigs: the nurturing, creative, and affectionate Jig of female language, and the manipulative, shallow, and hysterical Jig of male language. There are also two Americans: in the female language he is a cold, hypocritical, and powerful oppressor; in the male language he is a stoic, sensitive, and intelligent victim. ("Gender-Linked Miscommunication in 'Hills Like White Elephants,' " in *New Critical Approaches to the Short Stories of Ernest Hemingway*, ed. Jackson J. Benson [Durham: Duke University Press, 1990], p. 289.)

35.   Edwin J. Barton,"The Story as It Should Be: Epistemological Uncertainty in Hemingway's 'Cat in the Rain,' " *The Hemingway Review* 14 (Fall 1994): 75.

36.   Hemingway, *The Short Stories of Ernest Hemingway*, p. 161.

37.   *Ibid.*, p. 164.

38.   *Ibid.*, pp. 162-63.

39.   *Ibid.*, p. 164.

A Fugue for "The Killers"

Interrogating the Mirror:
Double-crossings in "The Killers"

> "Double-crossed somebody. That's what they kill them for."
> —*George*

Among the early critics who commented on the discrepancies between what *is* and what *seems* in "The Killers" was Edward C. Sampson, who pointed out in 1952[1] that very little in the story is what it appears to be: Henry's, which serves no alcoholic beverages, is a converted tavern run by George; Al and Max order *breakfast* at a *lunch* counter whose menu features *dinner*; the orders are mixed up; the time on the clock is wrong; Mrs. Bell runs Mrs. Hirsch's rooming house; and so on. Here Sampson let the matter rest, and most subsequent commentators have been content to see these discrepancies as framing the portrait of the disillusioned Nick Adams, who by story's end finds that the world of appearances conceals a terrifying reality beyond his imagination.[2]

There's more, however, to the narrative poetics of "The Killers" than a handful of discrepancies, which—significant as they are—don't explain the mechanics or, for that matter, the presence of complementarity throughout the story. "The Killers" is designed primarily to undercut its own epistemological reliability by raising questions concerning the nature of perception at the most fundamental levels of experience. The slippery world of the story is comprised of mutually exclusive and mutually interdependent appearances, in which oppositions, doublings, and epistemological erasures are the norm. In "The Killers," nothing is transcendent, nothing is certain: the characters shuttle continually between states of knowing and not knowing, thinking and not thinking, feeling and not feeling, wanting and not wanting—even their genders are confused on more than one occasion. In the end, Hemingway has cut out the phenomenological ground from under virtually everyone—Al, Max, Nick, George, Sam, Mrs. Bell, Ole Andreson, and, of course, the reader, who also finds him- or herself lost in a cloud of agnostic unknowing. This "cloud" is the story's true subject. As is the case throughout the complementarity group of Hemingway's short fiction, in "The Killers" subject and structure are synonymous.

The structure of "The Killers" consists of three complementary metapatterns. The multiple interconnections or fusions of the first two—which I'll label *Oppositions* and *Doublings*, respectively—combine to create a third metapattern, to be called *Double-crossings*. These three categories are themselves divided into several subsets—including cognition, affect, sense, and appetite—all of which comprise dual or multiple systems of meaning.

I

Oppositions

This metapattern features one set of complementary positives and one set of complementary negatives. The terms *positive* and *negative* don't exist independently of each other or in strictly binary opposition. Instead, their relationships are, in James Meriwether's illuminating phrase, "paradoxical, blurred, both oppositional and mutually supportive, [redolent] of radical difference and fundamental similarity."[3]

Cognition

In this category, Hemingway critiques reason as a reliable guide to the phenomenological realm of "The Killers." He accomplishes this task by foregrounding the following cognitive activities: *thinking, speaking, doing* and *knowing.* The first set of cognitions is illustrated by George's query of Al, "What's the idea?", and by Al's reply, "There isn't any idea." Typical of the second pair of positive and negative complementarities is Al's admonition to Max to "Shut up," counterbalanced by Max's command to George, "Talk to me, bright boy."[4] Oppositional doings are exemplified by Ole Andreson's "There ain't anything to do," and George's "that's a good thing to do."[5] Finally, the complementary status of knowing(s) is revealed in Nick's line, "I know it . . ." and Mrs. Bell's reply, "You'd never know it."[6]

Affect

In this subset may be found three mutually exclusive, yet interdependent, complementarities: *liking, feeling,* and *wanting.* The first complementarity emerges when Max tells Al, "I like him [George]," and is counterbalanced by Al's reply to Max, "I don't like it" (Max's banter with George).[7] Feeling is also rendered as a subset of positives (Max's "I got to keep bright boy amused, haven't I?"), and negatives (Mrs. Bell's "I'm sorry [Ole] don't feel well").[8] Wanting comprises the third affective oppositional entity: "Everything we want's the dinner, eh?" (Max to George), as opposed to Sam's "I don't want any more of that."[9]

144

Sense

The world according to three of the five senses—*seeing, hearing,* and *touch*—is also delineated in "The Killers" through a series of complementary oppositions. "Nick looked at the big man lying on the bed," is countered by "[Ole] Andreson did not look at Nick"; Al's reply to Max, "I can hear you all right," opposes Sam's "I don't even listen to it"; and the physically (and morally) insulated Al and Max eat "with their gloves on," while Nick "had never had a towel in his mouth before."[10]

Appetite

In addition to the ontological oppositions outlined above, "The Killers" features a series of complementarities represented by the physical appetites, namely *eating, drinking,* and *sexuality* (as defined by a series of gender-confusions). Like their cognitive activities, Al's and Max's eating habits also appear to be agnostic: "I don't know . . ." (Max to Al); "I don't know what I want to eat" (Al to Max).[11] When they finally decide, they're stymied in their attempts to order dinner at a lunch counter that appears to serve only breakfast. And when Al wants something alcoholic to drink, he is again met with opposition in the form of George's nonalcoholic bevo, ginger ale, and silver beer. The sexuality of predominantly male characters of the story is also inverted, as when Sam and Nick are described by Al as being tied up "like a couple of girl friends in a convent."[12]

II
Doublings

The second complementary metapattern in "The Killers" consists of doublings which, like the oppositions, inform the story's narration and dialogue from the very beginning. This counterbalancing of mutually exclusive and mutually identical phrases, words, and objects undermines the capacity of each individual metapattern to fully interpret the meaning(s) of appearances in the story.

Hemingway's predilection for repetition is well-documented. In chiding critics for over-simplistic assessments of this technique, Jackson J. Benson insists that, especially in Hemingway's short stories, repetition "is used in a number of different ways and often used subtly." Among the results of Hemingway's use of repetition, Benson adds, is a prose which offers the reader a "key to a complex of sensation—emotion."[13] Because Hemingway's critique of the appetites is exclusively oppositional, this "complex" is classified into just three of the four above-mentioned subsets: cognition, affect, and sense(s).

Cognition

Hemingway articulates the processes of thinking, speaking, doing and knowing in patterns of repetition as well: Max goads George, "What do you think . . .? What do you think . . .?"; Al chides Max, "You talk too much . . . You talk too much"; Ole Andreson doubles and re-doubles his despairing, "There ain't anything to do"; and Max and Al echo each other's "You never know."[14]

Affect

The affective states of liking, wanting, and feeling are also rendered in patterns of doublings. Max tells Al, "Bright boy is nice . . . He's a nice boy"; Sam insists, "I don't want any more of that . . . I don't want any more of that"; and Max tells George, "*You* don't have to laugh . . . *You* don't have to laugh at all, see?"[15]

146

Sense

Doublings of visual appearances include *persons* (Al and Max, "dressed like twins"); *menu items* (bacon and eggs, ham and eggs, liver and bacon); *objects* (Ole Andreson's two pillows); *action* (the brief appearances of two other people in the lunchroom); and *settings* (the two arc-lights Nick passes under on the way to Hirsch's). Visual perceptions are doubled too, as in "Max looked into the mirror . . . Max watched the mirror," or "Ole Andreson looked at the wall . . . He looked at the wall."[16] A twofold phenomenology of sounds also obtains: "Listen" (Al to George); "Listen" (George to Nick).[17] As for tactile sensations, Nick's close encounter with the towel in his mouth is also balanced by Sam's nervously feeling "the corners of his mouth with his thumbs."[18]

III

Double-crossings

Having schematized each metapattern, let me now turn to the structural relationship between the metapatterns. This relationship is a complex one and cannot be interpreted solely as an overarching system of binary oppositions. It's not a simple case of one, then the other, then one, then the other. At the center of the story's world of appearances is the *fusion* of doublings and oppositions. Because they double and invert at the same time, mirrors—including, of course, the one in Henry's that Max gazes into and speaks into—also embody complementarity. This dyadic principle of mirroring comprises the third metapattern of "The Killers."

Consider Al's bantering remark, "You never know," in response to Max's joke, "I suppose you were in a convent." Shockingly, this retort is doubled *and* countered by Max's sinister "You never know," spoken a few moments later in reply to George's question, "What are you going to do with us afterwards?"[19] Similarly,

Sam's "I don't like it" (having a towel stuffed in his mouth so he can't talk) is coupled with Al's "I don't like it" (referring to Max's habit of talking too much).[20] Another fusing of metapatterns occurs when Max tells George that they are killing Ole "just to oblige a friend," a remark that takes on even more frightening implications when George tells Max, "Your friend, Ole Andreson, isn't going to come."[21] In assigning the same sobriquet *friend* to Ole's arch enemy *and* to Ole himself, Hemingway alerts the reader to what a stricken Nick Adams will soon discover: in essence, Ole Andreson's death will be a suicide.

Yet another complementary fusion is provided by the aforementioned contrary pair of doings: "There ain't anything to do" (Ole), and "That's a good thing to do" (George).[22] Oppositional in terms of what they *say*, in terms of what they *mean* the statements are identical twins as well. Ole's remark springs from his refusal to confront the extreme horror of his situation, to get out of bed and do something about it; George's remark is directed at Nick's own response to Ole's predicament ("I can't stand to think about him . . .").[23] The "good thing to do" has, in fact, already been done by Ole, who *also* experiences extreme difficulty in thinking about it ("I can't make up my mind . . .").[24]

Note also the epistemological riddle, "What was it?" first uttered by Sam on entering the lunchroom from the kitchen.[25] Later, on seeing Nick enter his room at Hirsch's, Ole also asks, "What was it?"[26] In putting the same words of a man whose life will be spared in the mouth of one whose life is essentially over, Hemingway emphasizes Ole's awful isolation from his fellow beings. In this instance, the indefinite pronoun "it" does complementary double duty by signifying two utterly opposing human situations.

Of particular interest is the conjoining of dialogue near story's end that reveals the essence of Nick's ontological dilemma. This occurs when Nick recalls

George's earlier remark, "You better go see Ole Andreson," by telling Ole, "I better go back and see George."[27] The former statement is grounded in optimism (there's still time to warn Ole of his predicament), the latter in pessimism (Ole, it turns out, is indifferent to his predicament). Why, then, is it so important for Nick to return to Henry's to see George? Once again complementarity provides the answer. Because Nick is still anguishing between the two cognitive positions ("It's too damned awful . . ."), George offers him the story's ultimate agnostic advice: "Well, you better not think about it."[28] This, of course, from the bright boy who is described by Max earlier in the story as *a thinker*.

■ ■ ■

"The Killers" isn't merely *about* the aftermath of a double-cross with the hapless ex-boxer Ole Andreson caught in the middle; rather, "The Killers" *is* a double-cross with the reader himself caught in the cross-hairs of Ernest Hemingway's unusually intricate narratology. In the end, the story's three complementary metapatterns—Oppositions, Doublings, and Double-crossings—reveal "The Killers" in its true complexity as a supremely organic work of art, one of the most carefully wrought short fictions ever written.

———————

149

NOTES

1.	Edward C. Sampson, "Hemingway's 'The Killers,' " *The Explicator* 11 (October 1952): Item 2.

2.	Robert E. Fleming presents a far more thoroughgoing discussion of the "misunderstandings and false impressions" that toolmark "The Killers" than did Sampson. Fleming also positions the story's notorious discrepancies within the context of the Nick Adams stories as a whole. (Robert E. Fleming, "Hemingway's 'The Killers': The Map and the Territory," in *New Critical Approaches to the Short Stories of Ernest Hemingway*, ed. Jackson J. Benson [Durham: Duke University Press, 1990], p. 310).

3.	James Meriwether, "Chaos and Beckett's 'Core of Murmurs': Toward a Contemporary Theoretical Structure," *SubStance: A Review of Theory and Literary Criticism* 73 (1994): 105.

4.	Ernest Hemingway, *The Short Stories of Ernest Hemingway* (New York: Scribners, 1938), pp. 281, 283.

5.	*Ibid.*, pp. 288, 289.

6.	*Ibid.*, p. 288.

7.	*Ibid.*, pp. 284, 285.

8.	*Ibid.*, pp. 283, 288.

9.	*Ibid.*, pp. 280, 285.

10.	*Ibid.*, pp. 281, 283, 286, 287, 288.

11.	*Ibid.*, p. 279.

12.	*Ibid.*, p. 284.

13.	Jackson J. Benson, "Ernest Hemingway as Short Story Writer," in *The Short Stories of Ernest Hemingway: Critical Essays*, ed. Jackson J. Benson (Durham: Duke University Press, 1975), pp. 284, 286.

14.	Hemingway, *The Short Stories of Ernest Hemingway*, pp. 282, 284, 285, 287-88.

15.	*Ibid.*, pp. 284, 285, 281.

16.	*Ibid.*, pp. 282, 287.

17.	*Ibid.*, pp. 282, 286.

18.   *Ibid.*, p. 286.

19.   *Ibid.*, p. 284.

20.   *Ibid.*, pp. 285, 286.

21.   *Ibid.*, pp. 284, 285.

22.   *Ibid.*, pp. 287, 289.

23.   *Ibid.*, p. 289.

24.   *Ibid.*, p. 288.

25.   *Ibid.*, p. 282.

26.   *Ibid.*, p. 287.

27.   *Ibid.*, pp. 286, 288.

28.   *Ibid.*, p. 289.

Rosencrantz and Guildenstern are Alive

Critics have staked many claims for possible literary sources and analogues for the characters in "The Killers." John V. Hagopian and Martin Dolch see the story as a "grim and bitter parody on O. Henry's "The Ransom of Red Chief."[1] Arthur Waldhorn has suggested that the undertakers in Franz Kafka's *The Trial* anticipate Al and Max insofar as they are like Hemingway's hit men, "ridiculous and unreal" even as their mission is "serious and sinister."[2] Cleanth Brooks and Robert Penn Warren first proposed a useful Shakespearean analogue, arguing a generation ago that the landlady Mrs. Bell recalls "the Porter at Hell Gate in *Macbeth.*"[3] To my mind, the Shakespearean connection is also worth extending to Al and Max, who bear a striking resemblance to Rosencrantz and Guildenstern, the sleazy courtiers of *Hamlet*.[4]

In *Hamlet*, Guildenstern grudgingly informs the Prince that he and his partner were "sent for"; similarly, Max tells George in "The Killers" that he and Al plan to kill Ole Andreson "[j]ust to oblige a friend".[5] Both pairs act as instruments of the will of someone else to dispose of victims who are well aware of their terrible situations. Like Rosencrantz and Guildenstern, moreover, Al and Max willingly play the role of what Rosencrantz calls "the indifferent children of the earth" (II ii 222): all four are oblivious to the grim consequences of revenge, a vicious cycle which they enthusiastically (and literally) buy into. And both pairs are pleased to find a grisly humor in their calling. When Max tells Al, "Oh, what the hell . . . We got to keep amused, haven't we?",[6] he echoes Rosencrantz, whose lightsome mood prompts Hamlet's harsh demand, "Why did ye laugh then, when I said 'man delights not me?'" (II ii 303-309).

As critics of *Hamlet* have long noted, the felicitations of the King and Queen in Act II indicate that Rosencrantz and Guildenstern are ontologically interchangeable:

> Claudius: Thanks, Rosencrantz and gentle Guildenstern.
> Gertrude: Thanks, Guildenstern and gentle Rosencrantz. (II ii 33-34)

Like Shakespeare's courtiers, Al and Max are true doppelgängers, "dressed like twins."[7] The oft-cited scene in "The Killers" wherein George serves Al and the bacon and eggs ordered by Max, and Max the ham and eggs ordered by Al, is equivalent to the King's and Queen's chiasmatic greetings of Rosencrantz and Guildenstern. The ontological doubling of both pairs over extends to the scansion of their names—both Rosencrantz and Guildenstern consist of dactyls, while Al and Max are, of course, monosyllables.

Most telling of all is the doubling which also characterizes the dialogue in both texts. These repetitions, only a fraction of which I'll reproduce here, fall into two categories, as follows:

A

> Rosencrantz: Both your majesties
> Might, by the sovereign power you have of us,
> Put your dread pleasures more into command
> Than to entreaty.
> Guildenstern: But we both obey.
> And here give up ourselves in the full bent
> To lay our service freely at your feet,
> To be commanded. (II ii 27-32)

Both: We shall wait upon you. (II ii 265)

Max: "I don't know" . . . "What do you want to eat, Al?"
Al: "I don't know" . . . "I don't know what I want to eat."
Both: "You never know."[8]

B

Guildenstern: My Lord, I cannot [play the recorder].
Guildenstern: Believe me, I cannot. (III ii 338, 340)

Rosencrantz: What have you done, my lord, with the dead body?
Rosencrantz: My lord, you must tell us where the body is . . . (IV ii 4-5, 6, 24)

Al: "Got anything to drink?"
Al: "I mean you got anything to *drink*?"[9]

Max: "*You* don't have to laugh . . ."
Max: "*You* don't have to laugh at all, see?"[10]

In group A, both pairs of characters double the spirit or the letter of the language of their counterparts; in group B each character doubles *his own* words. The complementarity between these two sets of lexical repetitions is significant and deserves a closer look.

To demonstrate that *one* person is a rubber stamp, a sort of amoral clone who has no separate identity from another person, the authors choose to create *two* characters who are counterparts. Because the doubled lines spoken by each makes the characters redundant, they are subtracted, as it were, from two entities to one: 2=1. This is what happens in the doublings from group A. The situation is the same in the doublings from group B, except that in making his *own* lines redundant, each entity literally assigns to himself the ontological status of *no one*, and the numbers change to 1=0. The final equation, which distills the ontology of indifference to its very essence, is, therefore, 2=1=0. Perhaps Hemingway had this numerical principle in mind when he remarked to the critic Harvey Breit that he'd been "working in a new mathematics."[11] If so, Hemingway's new math wasn't really new at all, for what Hamlet says of Claudius applies to Rosencrantz and Guildenstern as well: "The King is a thing . . . of nothing" (IV ii 27, 29). Like Shakespeare's ontological twins, Hemingway's Al and Max are also double-talking personifications of complementarity: things of nothing.

NOTES

1.   It's of more than incidental interest, perhaps, that Tom Stoppard, the author of *Rosencrantz and Guildenstern are Dead*, freely acknowledged the influence of *"*The Killers" on his own writing. For Stoppard in his formative years, "The mysterious nature of the power of [Hemingway's] prose" in 'The Killers' especially helped to "make the boxer real and the gangsters real" to an extraordinary degree (Tom Stoppard, "Reflections on Ernest Hemingway," in *Ernest Hemingway: The Writer in Context*, ed. James Nagel [Madison: University of Wisconsin Press, 1984], p.22).

2.   Arthur Waldhorn, *A Reader's Guide to Ernest Hemingway* (New York: Farrar, Straus & Giroux, 1972), p. 61.

3.   Cleanth Brooks and Robert Penn Warren, "The Discovery of Evil: An Analysis of 'The Killers,' " in *Hemingway: A Collection of Critical Essays*, ed. Robert P. Weeks (Englewood Cliffs, N.J.: Prentice Hall, 1962), p. 117.

4.   Pointing out that both stories take place in a town called Summit, Hagopian and Dolch add,

   The words of one of the kidnappers to his companion, 'You must keep the boy amused,' also turn up in Hemingway's story: 'Well, I got to keep bright boy amused . . .' In both stories, moreover, the gangsters proceed in a decidedly theatrical manner and appear rather unreal—and in both stories their design fails (John V. Hagopian and Martin Dolch, *Insight I: Analysis of American Literature*, [Frankfurt am Main: Hirschgraben-Verlag, 1979], p. 99).

   A brief discussion of other sources and analogues for characters in "The Killers" may be found in Paul Smith, *A Reader's Guide to the Stories of Ernest Hemingway* (Englewood Cliffs, N.J.: Prentice Hall, 1989), pp. 138-53.

5.   Ernest Hemingway, *The Short Stories of Ernest Hemingway* (New York: Scribners, 1938), p. 287.

6.   *Ibid.*, p. 285.

7.   *Ibid.*, p. 280.

8.   *Ibid.*, pp. 279-80.

9.   *Ibid.*, p. 280.

10. *Ibid*, p. 281.

11. "Authors and Critics Appraise Works," *New York Times*, 3 July 1961, p. 7.

Nick and Ole Go to Court

"No," said the priest, "it is not necessary to accept everything as true, one must only accept it as necessary."

"A melancholy conclusion," said K. "It turns lying into a universal principle."

—Franz Kafka, *The Trial*

Only one counsel per side may address the court during the course of any motion, objection or other proceeding, unless permission is sought and granted by the court.

—Hon. Lance A. Ito, *Court Order*

Just the facts, ma'am.

—Joe Friday, *Dragnet*

In literature as in life, it often happens that any resemblance between the actual anatomy of a crime and courtroom justice is purely coincidental. Consider the sickening legal labyrinths of Chancery in Charles Dickens's *Bleak House*, or the trial of Dimitri for the brutal murder of his father in Dostoyevsky's *The Brothers Karamazov* (Dimitri's wrongful conviction and exile allow the real killer, Smerdyakov, who commits suicide anyway, to escape public censure). Most noteworthy of all, perhaps, is the arrest of Joseph K., the perplexed protagonist of Franz Kafka's *The Trial*, who never learns the true nature of his crime.

Closer to home, the egregious " mistrials" as depicted in William Faulkner's *The Hamlet*, Joseph Heller's *Catch-22*, and Robert Coover's *The Public Burning* have helped to establish black comedy as a subgenre in modern American fiction. What authors like Dickens, Dostoyevsky, Kafka, Faulkner, Heller, Coover and others share is a propensity for writing narratives *about* the myriad miscarriages of courtroom procedure. There are other, subtler ways, however, in which the fictions of literature and of the law bear witness, each to each, in the dock of the written word.

In the following scene from "The Killers," Nick Adams comes up to Hirsch's rooming house to tell Ole Andreson about the two hit men, Max and Al, who've arrived in the town of Summit to bump him off:

> Nick looked at the big man lying on the bed.
> "Don't you want me to go and see the police?"
> "No," Ole Andreson said. "That wouldn't do any good."
> "Isn't there something I could do?"
> "No. There ain't anything to do."
> "Maybe it's just a bluff."
> "No. It ain't just a bluff."

Speaking in the "same flat voice," Ole Andreson continues to fend off Nick's attempts to deny reality:

> Ole Andreson rolled over toward the wall.
> "The only thing is," he said, talking toward the wall,
> "I just can't make up my mind to go out. I been in here all day."
> "Couldn't you get out of town?"
> "No," Ole Andreson said, " I'm through with all that running around."
> ". . . Couldn't you fix it up in some way?"
> "No. I got in wrong."[1]

Compare this to a courtroom exchange from the O.J. Simpson trial of 1995,[2] as reported in the *Los Angeles Times* (the speakers are Deputy District Attorney Marcia Clark and Los Angeles Police Detective Ronald Phillips):

> "Did Mr. Simpson ask you how she was killed?" Clark asked.
> "No," Phillips answered.
> "Did he ask you when she was killed?" the prosecutor continued.

"No," he responded.
"Did he ask you if you had any idea who had done it?" Clark asked.
"No," the detective said.
"Did he ask you where it had occurred?" she questioned.
"No," the detective said.
Concluding, Clark asked: "Did he ask you anything about the circumstances of how his ex-wife had been killed?"
"No," Phillips answered one more time.[3]

The correspondences between these two brief scenes, one excerpted from a work of fiction, the other taken from a newspaper account of an actual event, are striking. The central figure in each quoted passage is an ex-athlete; both interrogations are concerned with murder, one past, one future; both are punctuated by the same monosyllabic responses, as funereal as a drum tattoo; both are characterized by an *apparent* flatness or atonality of style. And both passages raise profound questions concerning the necessity for illusion at the expense of truth in the conduct of human affairs. I'll return to this latter point in a moment.

As one would expect, the contrasts between the interrogations are equally striking. Both interlocutors are heading in opposite directions *in search of opposite truths*. Ms. Clark and her colleagues were engaged in an ongoing attempt to convince the jury that O.J. Simpson's boyish good looks, media image, and gentle courtroom demeanor cloaked the impulses of a double murderer whose words signified neither regret nor remorse. In "The Killers," the opposite is true: Nick Adams attempts to convince himself that Ole Andreson still has the killer instincts of the prizefighter he was, that his battered face signifies defiance. The housekeeper Mrs. Bell sees behind Ole's mask, however, telling the deflated Nick that Andreson, far from being a worthy opponent for the hit men Max and Al, is "just as gentle."[4] Thus, the mirror of each interrogation reverses the other, making of Ms. Clark and Nick Adams lexical Siamese twins. What, then, is the epistemological common bond that conjoins them?

160

To answer this question properly, let me juxtapose a second set of passages, each one constituting a definition of fiction. First, an ingredient from one of Hemingway's most famous recipes for the art of storytelling, the metaphor of the iceberg:

> If a writer of prose knows what he is writing about, he may omit things that he knows and the reader, if the writer is writing truly enough, will have a feeling of those things as strongly as though the writer had stated them. The dignity of movement of an iceberg is due to only one-eighth of it being above water.[5]

Second, an entry from *Black's Law Dictionary*:

> [a fiction consists of] an assumption or supposition of law that something which is or may be false is true, or that a state of facts exists which has never really taken place. . . . Something known to be false which is assumed to be true.[6]

We may begin a perusal of *both* of the above narratives as fictions from the perspective of Hemingway's doctrine of omissions. The deceptively simple scene in "The Killers" actually reveals the hidden inner lives of the two speakers more effectively than if, in Hemingway's idiom, "the writer had stated them." The cumulative No's, tellingly recorded in both Judge Lance Ito's courtroom and the fictional rooming house, here communicate a sense of Ole Andreson's profound depression more effectively than any grammatical markers or descriptive phrases possibly could. If Hemingway had added lines like *Ole Andreson clearly looked depressed to Nick,* or *Ole Andreson shook his head sadly,* or *Ole Andreson had simply given up,* the emotional effect would have been lost. In violating the Chekovian dictum that all guns in a literary work must go off, Hemingway shows that Ole Andreson is, in essence, already dead: the sawed off shotgun that Nick saw bulging in Al's overcoat, and that is never fired, is shockingly and appropriately redundant to the story's deeper horror.

The purpose of Ms. Clark's interrogation was to discover for the jury O.J. Simpson's actual frame of mind on being told of Nicole Brown Simpson's murder. Since the prosecution was seeking to prove that Simpson himself was the murderer, Clark's questions were meant to establish the damning *absence* of natural human curiosity about the circumstances of the event. In the strict parlance of *Black's Law Dictionary*, her intent was to show that true remorse "has never taken place." Ms. Clark's interrogatory strategy, therefore, was a (fortuitous) hybrid of Hemingway's formula for fiction and that of *Black's*. In establishing a lexical presence of absence, she turned to a cadenced sequence of questions that, because they were relentlessly repeated, built up powerful emotional momentum: *Did Mr. Simpson ask you? . . . Did he ask you? . . . Did he ask you? . . . Did he ask you? . . .* and so forth. Put another way, it was Ms. Clark's intent to have the jury feel the effect of a vicarious sting of remorse *by "listening" to what O. J. Simpson didn't say to Detective Phillips.*

This isn't to suggest that both passages are equally successful in achieving their desired effects. Ole Andreson's responses are more powerfully rendered than were Detective Phillips's, for instance, because they are precisely calibrated to counter each step in the wishful thinking of a naive adolescent ("Isn't there something I could do?"; "No. There ain't anything to do"; "Maybe it was just a bluff"; "No. It ain't just a bluff"). As a result, Nick's questions float freely in the lexical spacetime of Ole's metronomic "No's," untethered by narrative ballast like the *she continued* and *she saids* of the newspaper account. Leaner and purer than Ms. Clark's, Nick's lines might have been spoken by a character in a play. For Hemingway, as always, less is more.

Nonetheless, *both* sets of questionings produce what Hemingway also called a "sequence of motion and fact which made the emotion."[7] This sequence, or course, of lexical motion may lurk just beneath the conscious awareness of a fictional protagonist like Nick Adams; it may comprise the unwritten subtexts of an actual interrogation like the one conducted by Marcia Clark; and it may reveal a hidden dimension of meaning beneath the surface of legal injunctions like the court orders handed down by Judge Lance Ito during the Simpson trial. What overrules any individual fact or state of facts in both courthouse and rooming house is the complementary horror of murder that, felt *and* unfelt, is determined to be true.

NOTES

1.   Ernest Hemingway, *The Short Stories of Ernest Hemingway* (New York: Scribners, 1938), pp. 287-88.

2.   The murder trial of Orenthal James Simpson ended in acquittal on October 2, 1995.

3.   Jim Newton and Andrea Ford, "Simpson's Reaction to News of Death Recalled," *Los Angeles Times*, 17 February 1995, p. A1.

4.   Hemingway, *The Short Stories of Ernest Hemingway*, p. 288.

5.   Malcolm Cowley, "Introduction to *The Sun Also Rises*," in Ernest Hemingway, *Three Novels* (New York: Scribner's, 1960), p. xviii.

6.   Henry Campbell Black and Joseph R. Nolan, *Black's Law Dictionary: Definitions of Terms and Phrases of American and English Jurisprudence, Ancient and Modern*, 6th ed. (St. Paul, Minn.: West Publications, 1990), p. 751.

7.   Cowley, "Introduction to *The Sun Also Rises*," p. xviii.

SELECT BIBLIOGRAPHY

Albert, David Z. *Quantum Mechanics and Experience*. Cambridge, MA: Harvard UP, 1992.

Albright, Daniel. *Quantum Poetics: Yeats, Pound, Eliot, and the Science of Modernism*. New York: Cambridge UP, 1997.

Arnold, Matthew. "Stanzas from the Grande Chartreuse." *The Major Victorian Poets: Tennyson, Browning, Arnold*, edited by William E. Buckler. Boston: Houghton Mifflin Company, 1973, pp. 608-09.

Bakker, J. *Ernest Hemingway: The Artist as Man of Action*. Assan, N.V.: Van Gorcum & Company, 1972.

Barricelli, Jean-Pierre and Gibaldi, Joseph, eds. *Interrelations of Literature*. New York: Modern Language Association of America, 1982.

Barton, Edwin J. "The Story as It Should Be: Epistemological Uncertainty in Hemingway's 'Cat in the Rain.' " *The Hemingway Review* 14 (Fall 1994): 72-78.

Beegel, Susan F. "The Critical Reputation of Ernest Hemingway." In *The Cambridge Companion to Hemingway*, edited by Scott Donaldson. New York: Cambridge UP, 1996, pp. 269-99.

_____, ed. *Hemingway's Neglected Short Fiction: New Perspectives*. Tuscaloosa: U of Alabama P, 1989.

Beer, Gillian. "Problems of Description in the Language of Discovery." In *One Culture: Essays in Science and Literature*, edited by George Levine and Alan Rauch. Madison: U of Wisconsin P, 1987, pp. 35-58.

_____. "Wave Theory and the Rise of Literary Modernism." In *Realism and Representation: Essays on the Problem of Realism in Relation to Science, Literature, and Culture*, edited by George Levine. Madison: U of Wisconsin P, 1993, pp. 193-213.

Benert, Annette. "Survival Through Irony: Hemingway's 'A Clean, Well-Lighted Place.' " *Studies in Short Fiction* 11 (1974): 181-87.

Bennett, Warren. "Character, Irony, and Resolution: 'A Clean, Well-Lighted Place.'" In *The Short Stories of Ernest Hemingway: Critical Essays*, edited by Jackson J. Benson. Durham: Duke UP, 1975, pp. 261-69.

_____. " 'That's Not Very Polite': Sexual Identity in Hemingway's 'The Sea Change.' " In *Hemingway's Neglected Short Fiction: New Perspectives*, edited by Susan F. Beegel. Tuscaloosa: U of Alabama P, 1989, pp. 225-45.

Benson, Jackson J., ed. *New Critical Approaches to the Short Stories of Ernest Hemingway.* Durham: Duke UP, 1990.

_____. *The Short Stories of Ernest Hemingway: Critical Essays*. Durham: Duke UP, 1975.

_____. "Ernest Hemingway as Short Story Writer." In *The Short Stories of Ernest Hemingway: Critical Essays*, edited by Jackson J. Benson. Durham: Duke UP, 1975, pp. 272-310.

Black, Henry Campbell and Nolan, Joseph R. *Black's Law Dictionary: Definitions of Terms and Phrases of American and English Jurisprudence, Ancient and Modern.* 6th ed. St. Paul, MN: West Publications, 1990.

Blaser, Robin. "The Practice of Outside." In *The Collected Books of Jack Spicer*, edited by Robin Blaser. Los Angeles: Black Sparrow P, 1975, pp. 271-329.

Bluefarb, Sam. "The Search for the Absolute in Hemingway's 'A Clean, Well-Lighted Place' and 'The Snows of Kilamanjaro.' " *Bulletin of the Rocky Mountain MLA* 25 (1971): 3-9.

Bohm, David. *Wholeness and the Implicate Order.* London: Routledge and Kegan Paul, 1980.

Bohr, Niels. *Atomic Theory and the Description of Nature.* Cambridge: Cambridge UP, 1934.

Bowering, George, and Hogg, Robert. *Robert Duncan: An Interview*. Toronto: Coach House P, 1971.

Brenner, Gerry. "A Semiotic Inquiry into Hemingway's 'A Simple Enquiry.' " In *Hemingway's Neglected Short Fiction: New Perspectives,* edited by Susan F. Beegel. Tuscaloosa: U of Alabama P, 1989, pp. 195-207.

Broer, Lawrence. "Hemingway's 'On Writing': A Portrait of the Artist as Nick Adams." *Hemingway's Neglected Short Fiction: New Perspectives*, edited by Susan F. Beegel. Tuscaloosa: U of Alabama P, 1989, pp. 131-40.

Bronowski, J. *The Visionary Eye: Essays in the Arts, Literature, and Science*. Cambridge, MA: MIT P, 1978.

Brooks, Cleanth, and Robert Penn Warren. "The Discovery of Evil: An Analysis of 'The Killers.' " In *Hemingway: A Collection of Critical Essays*, edited by Robert P. Weeks. Englewood Cliffs, NJ: Prentice Hall, 1962, pp. 114-17.

Buckler, William E., ed. *The Major Victorian Poets: Tennyson, Browning, Arnold*. Boston: Houghton Mifflin Company, 1973.

Butterick, George F. *A Guide to* The Maximus Poems *of Charles Olson*. Berkeley: U of California P, 1978.

Byrd, Don. *Charles Olson's Maximus*. Urbana: U of Illinois P, 1980.

Capek, Milic. *The Philosophical Impact of Contemporary Physics*. New York: Van Rinehold Nostrand Company, 1961.

Capra, Fritjof. *The Tao of Physics*. New York: Bantam, 1977.

Christensen, Paul. *Charles Olson: Call Him Ishmael*. Austin: U of Texas P, 1979.

Davidson, Michael. " 'From the Latin *speculum*': the Modern Poet as Philologist." *Contemporary Literature* 28 (Summer 1987): 187-205.

DeFalco, Joseph. *The Hero in Hemingway's Short Stories*. Pittsburgh: U of Pittsburgh P, 1963.

Donaldson, Scott. "Preparing for the End: Hemingway's Revisions of 'A Canary for One.' " In *The Short Stories of Ernest Hemingway: Critical Essays*, edited by Jackson J. Benson. Durham: Duke UP, 1975, pp. 229-37.

_____, ed. *The Cambridge Companion to Hemingway*. New York: Cambridge UP, 1996.

Donley, Carol. "Modern Literature and Physics: A Study of Interrelationships." Ph.D. dissertation, Kent State University, 1975.

Duncan, Robert. *Bending the Bow*. New York: New Directions, 1968.

_____. " Ideas of the Meaning of Form." In *The Poetics of the New American Poetry*, edited by Donald Allen and Warren Tallman. New York: Grove P, 1973, pp. 195-211.

_____. "Towards an Open Universe." In *The Poetics of the New American Poetry*, edited by Donald Allen and Warren Tallman. New York: Grove P, 1973, pp. 212-25.

Eliot, T.S. *Collected Poems 1909-1962*. New York: Harcourt, Brace and World, 1963.

Ellmann, Richard and Charles Feidelson, eds. *The Modern Tradition*. New York: Oxford UP, 1965.

Evans, Ifor. *Literature and Science*. London: George Allen & Unwin, Ltd., 1954.

Fenton, James. "Going Half the Way." *The New York Review of Books*, 23 October 1997, pp. 32-34.

Fleming, Robert E. "Hemingway's 'The Killers': The Map and the Territory." In *New Critical Approaches to the Short Stories of Ernest Hemingway*, edited by Jackson J. Benson. Durham: Duke UP, 1990, pp. 309-13.

Flora, Joseph M. *Ernest Hemingway: A Study of the Short Fiction*. Boston: Twayne Publishers, 1989.

Gabriel, Joseph F. "The Logic of Confusion in Hemingway's 'A Clean, Well-Lighted Place.' " *College English* 22 (May 1961): 539-46.

Gleick, James. *Genius*. New York: Vintage, 1992.

Gould, Stephen Jay. *Dinosaur in a Haystack: Reflections in Natural History*. New York: Crown Publishing, 1995.

Grebstein, Sheldon Norman. *Hemingway's Craft*. Carbondale: Southern Illinois UP, 1973.

Greenberg, Robert A., ed. *Gulliver's Travels: An Annotated Text with Critical Essays*. New York: W.W. Norton, 1961.

Greenberg, Valerie D. *Transgressive Readings: The Texts of Franz Kafka and Max Planck*. Ann Arbor: U of Michigan P, 1990.

Gribbin, John. *Schrödinger's Kittens and the Search for Reality: Solving the Quantum Mysteries*. Boston: Little, Brown, and Company, 1995.

Haraway, Donna Jean. *Crystals, Fabrics, and Fields*. New Haven: Yale UP, 1976.

Hayles, N. Katherine. *The Cosmic Web: Scientific Field Models and Literary Strategies in the Twentieth Century*. Ithaca: Cornell UP, 1984.

_____. "A Manifesto: Re-defining Literature and Science." Modern Language Association Convention, New York, 29 December 1986.

Hemingway, Ernest. *The Short Stories of Ernest Hemingway*. New York: Scribners, 1938.

Holmesland, Oddvar. "Structuralism and Interpretation: Ernest Hemingway's 'A Cat in the Rain.' " In *New Critical Approaches to the Short Stories of Ernest Hemingway,* edited by Jackson J. Benson. Durham: Duke UP, 1990, pp. 58-72.

Hovey, Richard B. *Hemingway: The Inward Terrain*. Seattle: U of Washington P, 1968.

Huxley, Aldous. *Literature and Science*. New Haven: Leete's Island Books, 1963.

Ingman, Trisha. "Symbolic Motifs in 'A Canary for One.' " *Linguistics in Literature* 1 (1976): 35-41.

Jauch, J. M. *Are Quanta Real?* Bloomington: Indiana UP, 1973.

Johnson, Mark Andrew. *Robert Duncan*. Boston: Twayne Publishers, 1988.

Johnston, Kenneth G. *The Tip of the Iceberg: Hemingway and the Short Story*. Greenwood, FL: The Penkeville Publishing Co., 1987.

Jung, Carl. *The Portable Jung*, edited by Joseph Campbell. New York: Penguin, 1971.

Kazin, Alfred, ed. *The Portable Blake*. New York: Viking, 1946.

Kellert, Stephen H. *In the Wake of Chaos: Unpredictable Order in Dynamical Systems*. Chicago: U of Chicago P, 1993.

Levine, George, ed. *One Culture: Essays in Science and Literature*. Madison: U of Wisconsin P, 1987.

Lewis, Robert W. "Hemingway's Concept of Sport and 'Soldier's Home.' " In *The Short Stories of Ernest Hemingway: Critical Essays*, edited by Jackson J. Benson. Durham: Duke UP, 1975, pp. 170-80.

Lodge, David. "Analysis and Interpretation of the Realist Text: A Pluralistic Approach to Hemingway's 'A Cat in the Rain.' " *Poetics Today* 4 (Summer 1980): 5-22.

Lynn, Kenneth S. *Hemingway*. New York: Simon and Schuster, 1987.

Malkoff, Karl. *Escape from the Self*. New York: Columbia UP, 1977.

McHale, Brian. *Postmodernist Fiction*. New York: Methuen, 1987.

Meriwether, James. "Chaos and Beckett's 'Core of Murmurs': Toward a Contemporary Theoretical Structure." *SubStance: A Review of Theory and Literary Criticism* 73 (94): 95-108.

Merrill, Thomas F. *The Poetry of Charles Olson: A Primer*. Newark, DE: U of Delaware P, 1982.

Murdoch, Dugald. *Niels Bohr's Philosophy of Physics*. Cambridge: Cambridge UP, 1987.

Murfin, Ross C. "What is Deconstruction?" In James Joyce, *The Dead: Case Studies in Contemporary Criticism*, edited by Daniel R. Schwartz. Boston: St. Martin's P, 1994, pp. 206-15.

Nakjavani, Erik. "Repetition as Design and Intention: Hemingway's 'Homage to Switzerland.' " In *Hemingway's Neglected Short Fiction: New Perspectives*, edited by Susan F. Beegel. Tuscaloosa: U of Alabama P, 1989, pp. 263-82.

Newton, Jim and Andrea Ford. "Simpson's Reaction to News of Death Recalled." *Los Angeles Times*, 17 February 1995, p. A1.

O'Faolain, Sean. " 'A Clean, Well-Lighted Place.' " In *Hemingway: A Collection of Critical Essays*," edited by Robert P. Weeks. Englewood Cliffs, N.J.: Prentice Hall, Inc., 1962, pp. 112-13.

Olson, Charles. *The Maximus Poems IV, V, VI.* London: Cape Goliard/Grossman, 1968.

_____. *Human Universe and Other Essays*, edited by Donald Allen. New York: Grove P, 1963.

_____. *Letters for Origin*, edited by Albert Glover. New York: Cape Goliard, 1970.

_____. *The Maximus Poems*, edited by George F. Butterick. Berkeley: U of California P, 1983.

_____. "Projective Verse." In *The Poetics of the New American Poetry*, edited by Donald Allen and Warren Tallman. New York: Grove P, 1973.

_____. *Selected Writings*, edited by Robert Creeley. New York: New Directions, 1966.

Pattee, H.H. "The Complementarity Principle in Biological and Social Structures." *Journal of Social and Biological Structures* I (April 1978): 191-200.

Paul, Sherman. *The Lost America of Love.* Baton Rouge: Louisiana State UP, 1981.

_____. *Olson's Push.* Baton Rouge: Louisiana State UP, 1978.

Pizer, Donald, ed. *McTeague: A Norton Critical Edition.* New York: W.W. Norton, 1977.

Plotnitsky, Arkady. *In the Shadow of Hegel: Complementarity, History, and the Unconscious.* Gainesville, FL: UP of Florida, 1993.

Preminger, Alex and T.V.F. Brogan, eds. *The New Princeton Encyclopedia of Poetry and Poetics*. Princeton, NJ: Princeton UP, 1993.

Prigogine, Ilya. *From Being to Becoming*. New York: W. H. Freeman and Company, 1980.

Prigogine, Ilya and Isabelle Stengers. *Order Out of Chaos*. New York: Bantam, 1984.

Raynal, Maurice. *The Skira Modern Painting*. Trans. Stuart Gilbert. Switzerland: World Publishing, 1960.

Reid, Ian W. "The Plural Text: 'Passages.' " In *Robert Duncan: Scales of the Marvelous*, edited by Robert J. Berthoff and Ian W. Reid. New York: New Directions, 1979, pp. 161-80.

Reynolds, Michael. "*A Farewell to Arms*: Doctors in the House of Love." In *The Cambridge Companion to Hemingway*, edited by Scott Donaldson. New York: Cambridge UP, 1996, pp. 109-27.

Richards, I.A. *Poetries and Sciences*. New York: W.W. Norton, 1970.

Richardson, John Adkins. *Modern Art and Scientific Thought*. Urbana: U of Illinois P, 1971.

Riddell, Joseph N. *The Inverted Bell*. Baton Rouge: Louisiana State UP, 1974.

Ridley, B.K. *Time, Space, and Things*. New York: Penguin, 1976.

Rotella, Guy. "Comparing Conceptions: Frost and Eddington, Heisenberg, and Bohr." *American Literature* 59 (May 1987): 168-89.

Sampson, Edward C. "Hemingway's 'The Killers.' " *The Explicator* 11 (October 1952): Item 2.

Sanderson, Rena. "Hemingway and Gender History." In *The Cambridge Companion to Hemingway*, edited by Scott Donaldson. New York: Cambridge UP, 1996, pp.170-96.

Schrödinger, Erwin. "Discussions of Probability Relations Between Separated Systems." *Cambridge Philosophical Society Proceedings* 31 (1935): 555.

Serres, Michel. *Hermes: Literature, Science, Philosophy*. Baltimore: Johns Hopkins UP, 1982.

Shattuck, Roger. *The Innocent Eye*. New York: Farrar, Straus, and Giroux, 1984.

Shlain, Leonard. *Art and Physics: Parallel Visions in Space, Time, and Light*. New York: William Morrow, 1991.

Simmons, Kenith Levicoff. "Old Maids and the Domination of the Sea: Robert Duncan, Stan Brakhage, and Robert Kelly on the Self in Context." Ph.D. dissertation, University of Wisconsin, Madison, 1978.

Smiley, Pamela. "Gender-Linked Miscommunication in 'Hills Like White Elephants.' " In *New Critical Approaches to the Short Stories of Ernest Hemingway*, edited by Jackson J. Benson. Durham: Duke UP, 1990, pp. 288-99.

Smith, Julian. "'A Canary for One': Hemingway in the Wasteland." *Studies in Short Fiction* 5 (1968): 355-61.

Smith, Paul. *A Reader's Guide to the Stories of Ernest Hemingway*. Boston: G.K. Hall, 1989.

Spicer, Jack. "From the Vancouver Lectures." *Caterpillar* 12 (July 1970): 175-212.

_____. *The Collected Books of Jack Spicer*, edited by Robin Blaser. Los Angeles: Black Sparrow P, 1975.

Spilka, Mark. *Hemingway's Quarrel with Androgyny*. Lincoln: U of Nebraska P, 1990.

Stetler, Charles and Gerald Locklin. " 'A Natural History of the Dead' as Metafiction." In *Hemingway's Neglected Short Fiction: New Perspectives*, edited by Susan F. Beegel. Tuscaloosa: U of Alabama P, 1989, pp. 247-53.

Stevens, Wallace. *The Palm at the End of the Mind: Selected Poems and a Play*, edited by Holly Stevens. New York: Vintage, 1972.

Stock, Ely. "Nada in Hemingway's 'A Clean, Well-Lighted Place.' " *Midcontinent American Study Journal* 3 (Spring 1962): 53-57.

174

Stoppard, Tom. "Reflections on Ernest Hemingway." In *Ernest Hemingway: The Writer in Context*, edited by James Nagel. Madison: U of Wisconsin P, 1984, pp. 19-27.

Strehle, Susan. *Fiction in the Quantum Universe*. Chapel Hill: U of North Carolina P, 1992.

Strychacz, Thomas. *"In Our Time*, Out of Season." In *The Cambridge Companion to Hemingway*, edited by Scott Donaldson. New York: Cambridge UP, 1996, pp. 55-86.

Sypher, Wylie. *Loss of the Self in Modern Literature and Art*. New York: Vintage Books, 1962.

Unterecker, John. *A Reader's Guide to William Butler Yeats*. New York: The Noonday P, 1959.

Van Fraassen, Bas C. and Jill Sigman. "Interpretation in Science and the Arts." In *Realism and Representation: Essays on the Problem of Realism in Relation to Science, Literature, and Culture*, edited by George Levine. Madison: U of Wisconsin P, 1993, pp. 73-99.

Vitz, Paul C. and Arnold B. Glimcher. *Modern Art and Modern Science: The Parallel Analysis of Vision*. New York: Praeger Publishers, 1984.

von Hallberg, Robert. *Charles Olson: The Scholar's Art*. Cambridge, MA: Harvard UP, 1978.

Waldhorn, Arthur. *A Reader's Guide to Ernest Hemingway*. New York: Farrar, Straus, and Giroux, 1972.

Weeks, Robert P., ed. *Hemingway: A Collection of Critical Essays*. Englewood Cliffs, NJ: Prentice Hall, Inc., 1962.

Weingart, Peter and Sabine Maasen. "The Order of Meaning: The Career of Chaos as a Metaphor." *Configurations* 5 (Fall 1997): 463-520.

Wiley, Jr., John P. "Two Cultures—Never the Twain Shall Meet?" *Smithsonian* (October 1997): 20-22.

Williams, William Carlos. *Selected Essays of William Carlos Williams*. New York: New Directions, 1954.

Zukav, Gary. *The Dancing Wu Li Masters: An Overview of the New Physics*. New York: Bantam Books, 1979.

SUBJECT and NAME INDEX